RadioTimes
THE COMPANIONS

> "I think Amy Pond's the best companion ever. I honestly do"
>
> STEVEN MOFFAT, HEAD WRITER
>
> *RT APRIL 2010*

C000177919

FOREWORD

When you do a job for a year or so in your 20s, you don't expect it to haunt you for ever. But if you're a *Doctor Who* companion, things are different – this role defines careers.

I met the charming Anneke Wills (Polly, see page 100) at a *Doctor Who* convention almost 25 years after her brief mid-60s stint alongside William Hartnell and Patrick Troughton. Anneke had been paid to travel from her Californian home for a single afternoon's work – and her queue of waiting fans snaked onto the street.

Such is the pull of a companion. They're the nearest we'll ever get to entering the fantastic world of the Doctor. We measure ourselves against their every scream, every act of courage. And it doesn't go unmissed that they're often attractive members of the human species.

Radio Times has a proud tradition of bringing you the latest on each and every new recruit, with exclusive photoshoots and interviews, an unparalleled history collected here in all its glory. But we're far from done yet. Next year we'll see how the Tardis's first married couple get on: will Amy turn into a Stepford Wife? Unlikely. Will Rory man up?

You can't second-guess *Who's* brilliantly inventive head writer Steven Moffat, but I can reveal that *Radio Times* will be with them every step of the way.

Ben Preston *Editor Radio Times*

THE PROF AND ME
Ace (Sophie Aldred) and her
Professor, seventh Doctor
Sylvester McCoy, on location in
London in April 1988 for
Remembrance of the Daleks

"Sylv kept his scripts in
his pockets and always
at the last minute he gave
me all his long speeches.
He hated learning lines!"

SOPHIE ALDRED, *RT MAY 1996*

ACE
Sophie Aldred

Dates: 1987–89
Doctor: Sylvester McCoy

Ace (real name Dorothy) was working as a waitress on the planet Svartos when she met the Professor, as she called the Doctor. A troubled, feisty teenager from Perivale in London, Ace had been transported to Svartos by a time storm, and was only too happy to leave in the Tardis. Armed with a rucksack full of Nitro-9 explosives, she helped her mentor do battle with Daleks, Cybermen, robot clowns, vampiric Haemovores and a giant Bertie Bassett.

For seven years Ace had the distinction of being the last companion to be seen with the Doctor when the series was originally cancelled in 1989. "Come on, Ace," he said as they headed over the horizon. "We've got work to do…"

In *The Sarah Jane Adventures* (2010), Sarah revealed that she'd Googled former companions of the Doctor and discovered a "Dorothy something" running a company called **A** **C**haritable **E**arth (check the initials). Ace's organisation had raised billions.

IN THEIR OWN WORDS

"They needed someone who looked young for her age and could ride a motorbike, so I was just right. I do virtually all my own stunts. I've had to jump into a freezing river and beat up a Dalek with a baseball bat."
RT, November 1988

"For *Ghost Light* [right], we end up in a Victorian house and I have to wear a rather beautiful dress. I've decided I should blend in a bit more and not just wear my old black bomber jacket and badges all the time."
RT, September 1989

Arthur Darvill (Rory) on his favourite companion: "Ah well, if we're talking historically I'd say Ace. When I watched it when I was younger, she was always my favourite. I met Sophie Aldred the other week and she's brilliant. A lovely woman. So I've got to say her."
RT, November 2010

MEMORABLE MOMENT

Without doubt, Ace's finest hour came when she fearlessly laid into a Dalek with a baseball bat. (*Remembrance of the Daleks*, 1988)

> ## "I'm not really someone to sit around the Tardis and knit"
>
> SOPHIE ALDRED,
> *RT SEPTEMBER 1989*

ADAM MITCHELL
Bruno Langley

Dates: 2005 **Doctor:** Christopher Eccleston

"I always wanted to do a show with someone who was a rubbish companion," said the then show-runner Russell T Davies. Adam was the result. A young genius who catalogued alien artefacts for billionaire Henry Van Statten, he joined the Doctor and Rose for a trip to Satellite Five in the year 200,000. But his greed and selfish ambition proved to be his downfall. After the Doctor learnt that Adam had gleaned all the information he could about the technology of the future (in order to profit in his own time), he took Adam home for having flouted his time-travel code.

IN THEIR OWN WORDS

"The Collector [Henry Van Statten] catches the Doctor and Rose in his base and finds out the Doctor is an alien. So the Doctor becomes part of his collection. Then the Dalek starts to wake up... Daleks are so iconic. It's an image that's in your face from posters, books, videos. They're more than just monsters – they represent something. Danger."
RT, April 2005

MEMORABLE MOMENT

Adam's computer interface "infospike" surgery comes back to haunt him. With the click of his mother's fingers, Adam's forehead opens up – to her evident horror. *(The Long Game, 2005)*

> "The water creatures are terrifying. Their eyes really freak you out"
>
> LINDSAY DUNCAN
> *RT NOVEMBER 2009*

CAPTAIN ADELAIDE BROOKE
Lindsay Duncan

Dates: 2009 **Doctor:** David Tennant

In a series of specials building to the tenth Doctor's departure, David Tennant was teamed with distinguished actors who co-starred as one-off companions. After David Morrissey (Jackson) and Michelle Ryan (Christina) came Lindsay Duncan.

The self-assured, commanding Adelaide was a true pioneer: as the first woman to land on Mars, she was the natural choice to become head of the planet's Bowie Base One. The captain – a mother and grandmother – stayed professional while her crew became infected by a strange, water-producing life form.

Adelaide quickly formed a relationship of mutual respect with the Doctor, but was deeply affected by his knowledge of future events, ie the destruction of the base. When he interfered in the course of history and returned Adelaide and two other surviving crew members to Earth, she took her own life.

IN THEIR OWN WORDS

"My character Adelaide is an intelligent, motivated, dedicated professional who runs a research station on Mars. The water creatures are terrifying. Their eyes really freak you out. At first you're alienated by them, feeling that you want to get away. Then you become fascinated by the make-up job."
RT, November 2009

MEMORABLE MOMENT

An angry Adelaide points out her saviour's supreme arrogance: "This is wrong, Doctor! I don't care who you are! The Time Lord Victorious is wrong!"
(*The Waters of Mars*, 2009)

FAN BOYS *RT* snapped Matthew Waterhouse (aged 18) with *Doctor Who* writer Andrew Smith (19) on the *Full Circle* set in August 1980 – both were huge fans

ADRIC
Matthew Waterhouse

Dates: 1980–82
Doctors: Tom Baker, Peter Davison

The brilliant if spoddy mathematician from the planet Alzarius stowed away aboard the Tardis and accompanied the Doctor through his fourth-to-fifth regeneration. Though prone to sulking, the competitive Adric was determined to find a useful role to play among the Doctor's entourage. He died in an explosion when trying to regain control of a spaceship plunging towards Earth.

UP TO MISCHIEF
Adric caught thieving by Ivo (Clinton Greyn) in *State of Decay* (1980)

"Adric is mischievous, intelligent, inquisitive – he tends to stick his nose in where it's not wanted"

MATTHEW WATERHOUSE, *RT OCTOBER 1980*

Adric
MATTHEW WATERHOUSE

MEMORABLE MOMENT

That death scene... Unable to crack the last of a series of logic codes and therefore doomed to die, he says, "Now I'll never know if I was right." Cue silent end credits, a close-up of Adric's broken maths badge and a stunned audience. (*Earthshock*, 1982)

IN THEIR OWN WORDS

"Adric is mischievous, intelligent, inquisitive – he tends to stick his nose in where it's not wanted... I've been a fan of the show for as long as I can remember."
RT, October 1980

"I'd grown up with it and suddenly finding myself a part of it was really weird, but very exciting."
RT, 20th Anniversary Special, 1983

"Even after Adric died, he came back twice as a ghost. Peter [Davison] looked very pale – he couldn't believe he still hadn't got rid of me!"
RT, May 1996

TIME TEAM
Left: *RT* captured the youthful new Tardis quartet in September 1981 on location for *Castrovalva*. The newly regenerated fifth Doctor (Peter Davison) was aided – and sometimes challenged – by his youthful friends, Adric (Matthew Waterhouse), Tegan (Janet Fielding) and Nyssa (Sarah Sutton)

AMY POND
Karen Gillan

Dates: from 2010
Doctor: Matt Smith

Amelia Pond: the little girl with a crack in her bedroom wall, home alone but fearless. It's a first impression the Doctor will never quite shake – although he evidently *was* shaken (moments later for him, 15 years later for her) to be knocked out and handcuffed to a radiator by an all-grown-up Amy. In a skimpy WPC outfit, she unfurled her mane of red hair and announced, "I'm a kissagram!" Wowzah!

Amy and the actress who plays her, Karen Gillan, certainly made an impact with her Botticelli's Venus looks and 5ft 11in stature. She was a shoo-in at the Amy Pond auditions, held under the guise of *Panic Moon* (an anagram of "companion"). Once on screen, Gillan caused a minor uproar in some quarters of the press and with Mediawatch-UK, who questioned whether such a sexy companion belonged on teatime telly. Had they forgotten flesh-baring Leela?

What cannot be denied is that Amy is the most uninhibited female time traveller. Not for Amy the doe-eyed reticence shown by Rose and Martha. "Pond", as the Doctor likes to call her, propositioned him before her wedding and pinned him against his police box for a smooch.

But to the Doctor she'll always partly remain the seven-year-old he befriended just after his regeneration: Amelia Pond. "That's a brilliant name," he said. "Like a name in a fairy tale." Played with aplomb by Gillan's own cousin, **Caitlin Blackwood**, Amelia was like an icon from a children's classic: James who found a giant peach in his garden; the red-haired boy who watched for the Snowman…

For years, Amelia awaited the Time Lord's return, making up her own stories about the Raggedy Doctor. He became the subject of dolls, doodles and childhood games. "When I was seven I had an imaginary friend," she said. And then, just as 21-year-old Amy had almost put away those childish things, "The night before my wedding my imaginary friend came back." At last, Amy could explore her inner Wendy. On their first journey together, the Peter Pan-like Doctor held onto her ankle while she floated in space – still in her nightie – just outside the Tardis doors.

Amy is a modern woman who knows what she wants: the Doctor and all he can offer. She was less certain about her fiancé Rory – that is, until he was taken away from her. If at times she seemed a little cold and cut off from her feelings, well, wouldn't you be if a crack in time had left big blanks in your mind? Her parents had been erased from existence ("I don't have a mum and dad"). Only later, after Rory had been killed in the Silurian caves, did she realise how much she loved him. He was eventually restored to life and now they're married.

Who knows what fireworks 2011 will bring for Mr and Mrs Pond – the first newlyweds aboard the Tardis…

> "I guess there was a bit of an uproar. I just don't get it with the skirts. It's what any girl on the high street is wearing"
>
> KAREN GILLAN
> *RT JUNE 2010*

RadioTimes

EASTER FOOD | GORDON RAMSAY | NIGELLA LAWSON | JOHN TORODE | SOPHIE DAHL

3–9 April 2010 £1.10

radiotimes.com

EXCLUSIVE

ALL NEW WHO

Matt Smith and Karen Gillan
welcome you aboard the new Tardis
Every episode previewed by Steven Moffat

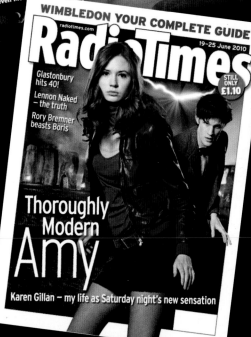

WIMBLEDON YOUR COMPLETE GUIDE

RadioTimes

radiotimes.com

19–25 June 2010

STILL ONLY £1.10

Glastonbury hits 40!

Lennon Naked – the truth

Rory Bremner beasts Boris

Thoroughly Modern Amy

Karen Gillan – my life as Saturday night's new sensation

TOO HOT FOR TEATIME?
Amy's look and modern attitude to sex
raised temperatures and grabbed headlines

'IME LORD'S STUNNING NEW ASSISTANT

I'm the sexiest sidekick Dr Who's

SHE'S the flame-haired
temptress who'll be
helping Dr Who with his
sonic screwdriver.

Doctor Ooooh!

How the Time Lord's saucy, short-skirted
new companion sent viewers into orbit

"Amy's not going to mope around when the Doctor's not there – she's going to do her own thing, whether it's fighting monsters in strange new worlds or just getting on with her life in her own village"

KAREN GILLAN, *RT JUNE 2010*

HOT STUFF
Karen Gillan debuted in *Doctor Who* in 2008 as a soothsayer in *The Fires of Pompeii* – bet she didn't prophesy her future role in *Doctor Who*!

15

THE LITTLE GIRL WHO WAITED
Amelia Pond (top) was all grown up by the time the Doctor popped back (above) with an apple with a face carved into it. In real life, the actresses Caitlin Blackwood and Karen Gillan are cousins

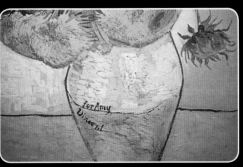

NEW DIMENSIONS
In this *RT* exclusive, Karen Gillan and Matt Smith went before the cameras in March 2010 to show off the new Tardis set, constructed at Upper Boat Studios just outside Cardiff

MEMORABLE MOMENT

In an art gallery, Amy weeps for the tortured soul of Vincent van Gogh, but is cheered to discover that her friend has dedicated an oil painting to her. She reflects on what might have been, on the marriage proposal she turned down. "Our kids would have had very, very red hair," she says. "The ultimate ginge. Brighter than sunflowers." (*Vincent and the Doctor,* 2010)

"She's funny and clever and gorgeous and sexy. Or Scottish, which is the quick way of saying it"

STEVEN MOFFAT, *RT APRIL 2010*

IN THEIR OWN WORDS

"She's quite a feisty girl. Amy's not so much in awe of the Doctor. It's a really interesting dynamic because she doesn't just listen to any old rubbish – Amy gives as good as she gets. Romance isn't the driving force behind their relationship. It's much deeper – more like a connection between two lost souls who have found each other."
RT, April 2010

"Her style is very thrown together – quite different from mine. But she's a cool girl. Much cooler than me."
RT, April 2010

Steven Moffat: "We saw some amazing actresses for the part, but when Karen came through the door, the game was up. She's funny and clever and gorgeous and sexy. Or Scottish, which is the quick way of saying it."
RT, April 2010

On her new-found fame: "It's weird, but nice-weird. Of course, it's strange to wake up and find journalists staking out your house, but no one's been nasty. I went on the Tube the other day, at night, and no one looked twice. Bit of an anticlimax, really. I can use public transport depending on the time of day – if there were a lot of children around, it would probably be impossible. But that's not something you can worry about. I mean, *Doctor Who* is just the most brilliant job."
RT, June 2010

"The one thing I never wanted to do with Amy was to base her on any kind of formula, to conform to what works or what has worked in a companion; you know, the whole, likeable, girl-next-door business. Amy is likeable, I hope, but she's not ordinary. She's quite complicated and there are layers to explore. So I was taking a few risks with her and I think it works."
RT, June 2010

On her sexy clothes: "Yeah, I guess there was a bit of an uproar and I really didn't see that coming. I just don't get it with the skirts. It's what any girl on the street is wearing. I mean, Amy's not a schoolgirl. She's 21, pretty much the same age as me, and we all wear stuff like this."
RT, June 2010

On Amy's relationship with the Doctor: "Ultimately, I think they're like brother and sister – he's quite protective of her and they bicker like siblings do, but ultimately they'd do anything for each other. Sometimes, though, she's attracted to him, and that's when things get a bit more complicated. I think he basically still sees her as the little Amelia he met when she was seven. So when she kisses him, he's like, 'Ooh, this is all wrong,' and she's like, 'Why isn't he reciprocating?' So she pushes it a bit, just to test her power. But in the morning, she's back to being his annoying little sister again."
RT, June 2010

COOL KAREN

A striking fashion shoot
with Karen Gillan – even
Amy wouldn't go into time
and space wearing this!

ASTRID PETH
Kylie Minogue
Dates: 2007
Doctor: David Tennant

In a headline-grabbing coup for *Doctor Who*, Australian pop diva Kylie Minogue was cast opposite David Tennant for a one-off appearance in the 2007 Christmas special, *Voyage of the Damned*. The former *Neighbours* star was delighted to be offered a brief return to acting. No singing required.

With a staid hairdo but in sexy boots and stockings, she played Astrid, a waitress aboard the space liner *Titanic*, who opened her heart to the Doctor. A citizen of planet Sto without any family, Astrid was later described by the Time Lord as "the woman who looked at the stars and dreamt of travelling". When events began to unfold like a disaster movie, Astrid proved a brave associate, wiping out a number of the lethal robotic Host before dying in an attempt to rescue the Doctor.

A teleport bracelet partially saved her life force as a spectral suspension of atoms. The Time Lord released her into space as glittering stardust with the words, "Now you can travel for ever. You're not falling, Astrid. You're flying."

TITANIC PAIRING
Main picture: for the *RT* cover, Kylie Minogue and David Tennant echoed the famous image from the movie *Titanic*. No such scene occurred in the episode

"At the read-through I tried to look cool, but was petrified"

KYLIE MINOGUE,
RT DECEMBER 2007

IN THEIR OWN WORDS

"I've a low boredom threshold and jump at opportunities. *Doctor Who* goes back to my roots as an actress. At the read-through, I tried to look cool but was petrified. Then on my first day of filming, I realised I was in my spiritual home. I've a lot of affection for Astrid. She's a waitress on the *Titanic*, a dreamer, alone, and wants to travel. Perhaps that's like me when I was younger, but I had opportunities and she's still struggling."
RT, December 2007

David Tennant: "Everyone got very twittery when we heard Kylie was coming. There were all sorts of members of the art department explaining why they had to be on set. Then she comes in and is refreshingly normal and fun and easy and none of the things that I suppose a big pop diva has every right to be."
RT, December 2007

MEMORABLE MOMENT

Heroically coming to the Doctor's rescue, Astrid uses a forklift truck to pick up Max Capricorn, the wicked, motorised owner of the *Titanic*. She sends him hurtling into the ship's engine core — but perishes in the process herself.
(*Voyage of the Damned*, 2007)

BARBARA WRIGHT
Jacqueline Hill

Dates: 1963–65
Doctor: William Hartnell

"Wait in here, please, Susan. I won't be long" – *Doctor Who's* inauspicious but very first words were uttered in a school corridor by history teacher Miss Barbara Wright. It was London 1963, and Barbara's misgivings about her strange pupil, Susan, would kick-start the world's longest-running sci-fi series. Barbara and her Coal Hill School colleague Ian Chesterton were abducted by Susan's grandfather, the Doctor, and initially made for unwilling travellers in the Tardis.

Rancour and terror gradually gave way to trust and fondness. The amoral, selfish first Doctor was soon beguiled by Barbara's humanity and intuition, telling her, "As we learn about each other so we learn about ourselves." Historian Barbara made a perfect companion for those early journeys into Earth's past, encountering Marco Polo (right) and Saladin, spying on Napoleon – she was even pursued by an amorous Nero. She and Ian eventually made it back to Earth two years later in a Dalek timeship.

Jacqueline Hill returned to *Who* in Tom Baker's final season to play Lexa in *Meglos* (1980). She died in 1993. In *The Sarah Jane Adventures* (2010), Sarah revealed that Ian and Barbara were married and living in Cambridge as professors. "Rumour has it, they've never aged. Not since the 60s."

IN THEIR OWN WORDS

Jacqueline Hill was the first-ever member of the regular cast to speak to *RT* about *Doctor Who*: "I don't regard it as fantasy. The notion of how the travellers reach their destination may be fantastic, but when they get there, they're involved in reality…" She and her husband, director Alvin Rakoff, had no offspring at the time, but, "Our best friends have two children and one of them is usually ready to tell me when I've gone wrong."
RT, May 1964

"I left when they dropped me in Hyde Park [sic, it was actually White City] and sent me back to school as if it was yesterday." Now she returns in *Meglos* "with promotion, as a high priestess. It's nice to know that you get nearer to heaven as you get older."
RT, September 1980

William Russell (Ian): "I loved Jackie. She was a very attractive woman, and we had lots of shared memories because we were both Midlanders. She'd been a Cadbury's girl at Bourneville. We'd often talk in a Brummy accent. At the end of our time on *Doctor Who*, I said to Jackie, 'Let's do *Separate Tables*, the Terence Rattigan play.' It was a chance for both of us and we did a little theatre tour. We weren't crying to be leaving. I'm always looking forward to the next experience. You have to as an actor."
RT, November 2010

Radio Times
SIXPENCE

FEBRUARY 22—28

BBC tv Sound

DR. WHO
The four travellers in time and space return to Earth for a new adventure beginning on Saturday on Television
SEE PAGE 7

HUGH AND I
Leol-Scomb Terry Scott and Hugh Lloyd as they resume their televised series in Detections on Valentine
PAGE 6

BENNY HILL
Laugh—with the more Benny in his new show on Sunday afternoon in the Light
SEE PAGE 15

ERIC SYKES
Laugh—with Liz and Hattie Jacques as they begin a series in Television on Tuesday
PAGE 27

IN THE LIGHT AND ON TELEVISION
World Heavyweight Championship
SONNY LISTON v. **CASSIUS CLAY**
SEE PAGE 29

IN THE LIGHT
The British, British Empire, and European Championship
HENRY COOPER v. **BRIAN LONDON**
SEE PAGE 21

PLUNGED INTO DANGER

Above: Barbara (Jacqueline Hill) was the first companion to meet a Dalek, in a classic cliffhanger from 1963

Main picture: *RT* was on set at Lime Grove Studios in January 1964 for *Marco Polo,* an early classic that garnered *Doctor Who's* first *RT* cover (inset above).
L–R: Ping-cho (Zienia Merton), Barbara, Polo (Mark Eden), Susan (Carole Ann Ford), Tegana (Derren Nesbitt)

MEMORABLE MOMENT

Barbara finds herself hailed as the reincarnation of the high priest Yetaxa. Aware of the doom facing Aztec society, she's determined to use her new powers to put a stop to human sacrifice. (*The Aztecs,* 1964)

"The notion of how the travellers reach their destination may be fantastic, but when they get there, they're involved in reality…"

JACQUELINE HILL, *RT May 1964*

POSITIONS, PLEASE
The Doctor (William Hartnell), Vicki (Maureen O'Brien), a recumbent Ian (William Russell) and Barbara (Jacqueline Hill) encountered a Dalek and two golden Aridians. This was a specially posed publicity shot for *The Chase* (1965) — no such scene occurred in the televised episodes

WRIGHT STUFF
Top: Barbara befriended a Menoptra in *The Web Planet*, and made it onto the *RT* cover in 1965. Below: Jacqueline Hill returned to *Doctor Who* in 1980. In *Meglos*, playing zealous Tigellan priestess Lexa, she met Lalla Ward, who played companion Romana

BEN JACKSON
Michael Craze

Dates: 1966–67
Doctors: William Hartnell, Patrick Troughton

Cockney seaman Ben was a moody, handsome hero, despondent at being posted ashore from his ship, HMS *Teazer*. He cheered up considerably after hooking up with Polly in a Swinging Sixties nightclub. They helped the first Doctor to foil a plot involving the War Machines, then used Dodo's key to come aboard the Tardis.

Ben and Polly were the first companions to encounter the Cybermen as well as being the first to witness the Doctor changing his form. They tackled 17th-century pirates and smugglers, Highlanders, Daleks and Macra... Then, after an encounter with the bodysnatching Chameleons, the attractive pair realised that, quite by chance, they had returned to London on the same day they'd left – and decided to stay.

Michael Craze eventually gave up acting to run a pub and died in 1998. (*Little Britain* honoured him in 2003 with Matt Lucas playing theatrical agent Sir Michael Craze.)

IN THEIR OWN WORDS

"I played Ben, the cockney merchant seaman, who came into the series at the same time as Polly. Ben wasn't as arrogant as I'd like to have made him, but he was a tough bloke. Anneke [Wills, playing Polly] and I spent much of the time being chased by Cybermen, who'd just been introduced. It's tough making your mark when you're surrounded by a bunch of scene-stealing monsters.

"Once I was captured by pirates. They were supposed to make me walk the plank. They suspended me over the edge of the big water tank at Ealing Studios and then the plank was whipped away from under my feet. It was terrifying. The Doctor came to the rescue eventually, but not before I'd got thoroughly soaked."

RT, 10th Anniversary Special, 1973

NO ESCAPE
Six years after they'd left *Doctor Who*, Michael Craze and Anneke Wills were reunited for a photoshoot – with the Cybermen in Norfolk – for an *RT* special celebrating the programme's tenth anniversary

"Anneke and I spent much of the time being chased
by Cybermen, who'd just been introduced"

MICHAEL CRAZE, *RT 1973*

FROSTY RECEPTION
"How dare you follow me into the Tardis!" roared the Doctor (William Hartnell) at Ben (Michael Craze) and Polly (Anneke Wills) in *The Smugglers* (1966)

MEMORABLE MOMENT
Ben and Polly narrowly escape the hideous crabs controlling the Colony. Moments later, however, a brainwashed Ben strains to deny their existence. "There were no such creatures. There are no such things as Macra!" (*The Macra Terror*, 1967)

"Ben wasn't as arrogant as I'd like to have made him"

MICHAEL CRAZE, *RT 1973*

POWERFUL PAIR
Riverside Studios, October 1966: *RT* photographed Anneke Wills and Michael Craze during camera rehearsals for *The Power of the Daleks*, the debut story of second Doctor Patrick Troughton

RT 37 0.60

"I've grown very fond of the Brig, as we call him. I want him to be a human being, not a cipher"

NICHOLAS COURTNEY, *RT 1973*

BRIGADIER LETHBRIDGE STEWART
Nicholas Courtney

Dates: 1968–75, 1983, 1989, 2008
Doctors: Patrick Troughton, Jon Pertwee, Tom Baker, Peter Davison, Sylvester McCoy

Nicholas Courtney has the distinction of performing alongside more Doctors than any other actor. He even appeared with first Doctor William Hartnell in 1965 as a kind-of companion, Space Security agent Bret Vyon, who was shot by his own sister, Sara Kingdom (see page 122).

Courtney was pressed into service again in the classic second Doctor story *The Web of Fear* as Colonel Lethbridge Stewart in a battle against the Yeti. Promoted to Brigadier, he became the Time Lord's most enduring male associate, featuring in more than 100 episodes across four decades.

As head of the British branch of Unit (United Nations Intelligence Taskforce), he provided a base for the third Doctor during his long exile to Earth. Unusually for a military man, the Brig instinctively trusted in the Time Lord and his outlandish claims, albeit favouring artillery over diplomacy as they fended off everything from Autons to Zygons.

The Brig preferred to draw a veil over his private life. It wasn't until *Planet of the Spiders*, when he'd been in the series six and a half years, that viewers finally heard his first name – Alistair. We also learnt that he'd once had a dalliance in Brighton with "a young lady called Doris" (eventually to become his wife).

He later became a teacher at a public school, meeting the fifth Doctor in 1983, and has been called out of retirement several times since, most recently in 2008 (elevated to Sir Alistair) for *The Sarah Jane Adventures*.

MAN OF ACTION
Top: The military mind of the Brigadier (Nicholas Courtney) was often at odds with the scientific approach of the third Doctor (Jon Pertwee), as this scene from *Terror of the Autons* (1971) encapsulates
Above: *RT* reunited a tache-less Brig with Liz Shaw (Caroline John) in 1973 for its *10th Anniversary Special*

33

MEMORABLE MOMENT

At last – after five years in the series and to viewers' delight – a bemused Brigadier steps aboard the Tardis. "So *this* is what you've been doing with Unit funds and equipment all this time," he huffs. (*The Three Doctors,* 1973)

IN THEIR OWN WORDS

"I'm not really an Army man, though I did my National Service as a private. I've grown very fond of the Brig, as we call him. I want him to be a human being, not a cipher. I try to make him endearing and to get some fun into the action, the sort of humour that arises out of character and situation. I don't want him to look a twit. I think he appears genuine. At least, a brass hat from the War Office once told a producer, 'He's exactly like our lot!' "
RT, 10th Anniversary Special, 1973

"The Brigadier sees everything straightforwardly. His military mind is a good foil to the Doctor's scientific one. The Doctor genuinely likes him. The Brigadier brings something to the stories set on Earth. There is something extra scary when the monsters are creeping up your back yard."
RT, January 1983

"I started with William Hartnell (not as the Brigadier), and ended with Sylvester McCoy. Who's best? Well, as the Brig was heard to say, 'They're splendid chaps – all of them!' "
RT, May 1996

"The Brig's retired, tending his garden, waiting for the call to arms from the Doctor. If the script were right, I'd love to do one story. It'd be great fun. I want a story where they kill me off."
RT, May 2008

"I have a lot of loyal fans and they're all rather delighted that I've been pulled out of retirement. I mean, it doesn't seem all that long ago that the Unit clan was all together. He's got fatter. He's a very decent chap, the Brig. Very trustworthy. That's why the Doctor liked him."
RT, December 2008

GOOD OLD NICK

Top left: the Brig inside the Tardis with second Doctor Patrick Troughton and Jo (Katy Manning) in *The Three Doctors* (1973)

Top right: in his first *Who* role, agent Bret Vyon in *The Daleks' Master Plan* (1965)

Above: absorbing fourth Doctor Tom Baker's wild hypotheses in *Terror of the Zygons* (1975), with Benton (John Levene) and Huckle (Tony Sibbald)

Left: aged 78, Nicholas Courtney co-starred with old chum Elisabeth Sladen in a 2008 entry of *The Sarah Jane Adventures*

ALL ABOARD
For *Doctor Who's* unofficial 200th story, *Planet of the Dead*, David Tennant, Michelle Ryan and a No 200 bus fetched up in sunny Dubai. However, the *RT* cover and main image here are montages shot in a chilly studio in Cardiff

LADY CHRISTINA DE SOUZA
Michelle Ryan

Dates: 2009
Doctor: David Tennant

From *EastEnders*, via *The Bionic Woman*, Michelle Ryan had a one-off stint as an aristocratic cat burglar who met the tenth Doctor on a London double-decker after she'd stolen the Cup of Athelstan. When the bus passed through a wormhole to the planet San Helios, Christina and the Doctor had encounters with insectoid Tritovores and a destructive swarm of stingray-like aliens before returning the bus passengers to their own place and time.

Despite the fact that they were clearly kindred spirits, the Doctor turned down Christina's pleas to travel with him because he didn't want to lose another companion.

IN THEIR OWN WORDS

"I was probably the only person who thought the sandstorm was great. Like Christina, I love extremes. This girl is me! I don't find myself particularly sexy. But I guess being curvy, you put on certain clothes and they cling and it's inevitable. When I put on the catsuit, the costume girls were like, 'Wow!' Even Russell T Davies said, 'Well, the boys are gonna have fun!'"
RT, April 2009

David Tennant: "She's very easy-going. She's been to Hollywood and back, but is untouched by pretension or actors' lunacy, which others in her position might be. She's a delight to have around and seems to be having fun. She loves all the throwing-yourself-around stuff."
RT, April 2009

MEMORABLE MOMENT

Going against the Doctor's advice, the catsuited Christina plunges down a shaft to retrieve a crystal that powers the Tritovore spaceship. "The aristocracy survives for a reason... We're ready for anything!"
(*Planet of the Dead*, 2009)

"When I put on the catsuit, the costume girls were like, 'Wow!' Even Russell T Davies said, 'Well, the boys are gonna have fun!'"

MICHELLE RYAN, *RT APRIL 2009*

"She's been to Hollywood and back, but is untouched by pretension or actors' lunacy"

DAVID TENNANT, *RT APRIL 2009*

DRESSING UP
Dodo (Jackie Lane) had fun exploring the Tardis wardrobe before arriving on *The Ark* (1966) with the Doctor (William Hartnell) and Steven (Peter Purves)

5

RT300.--

DODO CHAPLET
Jackie Lane
Dates: 1966
Doctor: William Hartnell

Dodo (Dorothea) barged into the Tardis on Wimbledon Common thinking it was a real police box. The Doctor took to the mischievous orphan at once, remarking on her likeness to his granddaughter, Susan, although Dodo's use of catchy 60s words like "fab" grated on his nerves.

Her accent wavered between Mancunian and plummy from one episode to the next. (Behind the scenes, BBC executives changed their minds about how Dodo should speak.) After a handful of adventures, she had an ignominious off-screen exit, sending the Doctor a message via Polly and Ben that she was staying in present-day London.

IN THEIR OWN WORDS

"I'm only five feet tall and I have a girlish face so I began to get stuck with children's parts, and once I realised that I wasn't going to play Hedda Gabler or Cleopatra, acting lost its appeal."
RT, 20th Anniversary Special, 1983

MEMORABLE MOMENT
Tombstone, 1881: a brave but foolhardy Dodo comes between Johnny Ringo (Laurence Payne) and Doc Holliday (Anthony Jacobs) during the gunfight at the OK Corral. (*The Gunfighters*, 1966)

KEEPING AN EYE

A Monoid attends Dodo in *The Ark* (1966)

DONNA NOBLE
Catherine Tate

Dates: 2006–2010
Doctor: David Tennant

"You're the most important woman in the whole of creation," Rose would one day tell Donna. Initially, however, the gobby temp from Chiswick was the most reluctant time traveller.

She surprised everyone at the end of *Doomsday* (2006) when she suddenly appeared aboard the Tardis in a bridal gown – Catherine Tate was then better known for her BBC comedy series. Once they'd dispatched the Empress of the Racnoss, Donna bid the Doctor farewell, but soon realised her mistake and spent months tracking him down.

After a comical reunion at Adipose Industries (above), she became the Doctor's best buddy and developed an unexpectedly empathic side to her personality. She saved the whole of reality from destruction by Davros and the Daleks, and became the "Doctor/Donna" after assimilating the Time Lord's DNA. To save her life, the Doctor had to erase her memories and return Donna to her former life of self-absorption.

We last saw her on her second wedding day when the Doctor presented the Noble family with a winning Lottery ticket.

PARTNERS IN CRIME
Right: Sarah Lancashire (villainous Miss Foster), David Tennant and Catherine Tate in one of four *RT* cover montages launching series four in 2008

IN THEIR OWN WORDS

On her shock arrival at the end of *Doomsday*: "They said it was the first time a secret hasn't leaked out of *Doctor Who*. So we were just delighted that no one was expecting me to turn up in the Tardis. It was definitely cloak-and-dagger. It was a closed set and I booked into hotels under three different names."
RT, December 2006

Russell T Davies: "When the Doctor offered her a place aboard the Tardis she said no. I've always imagined Donna's reaction when she woke up on Boxing Day. 'I said what?!' She's realised that life as a temp in Chiswick doesn't quite compare to adventures in time and space. Now she's determined to put that right."
RT, April 2008

"Donna's quite a force of nature, so she doesn't really take no for an answer. In *The Runaway Bride* all she wanted to do was get away from him; then, as it turns out, all she wants to do is be with him. They really rounded Donna out from being a shouting fishwife to someone who's quite vulnerable and emotional."
RT, April 2008

Russell T Davies: "She brings out the Doctor's sense of fun, but she's brilliant at bringing him down to earth. I think Donna's the first one to truly understand him. He can be completely honest with her, admitting when he's scared, or lost, or powerless."
RT, June 2008

On magazine cover:

THE ULTIMATE DIGITAL TV AND RADIO GUIDE

BEST FOR
YOU KNOW WHO!

RadioTimes

www.radiotimes.com
1 OF 4 COLLECTABLE COVERS

5–11 APRIL 2008 £1

POLICE PUBLIC BOX

PLUS
Russell T Davies's
exclusive guide
to the new
series!

Sarah
Lancashire
as Miss Foster

RT EXCLUSIVE

THE STARS
ARE COMING OUT...
Look who's joining David Tennant and
Catherine Tate for the return of *Doctor Who!*
Saturday BBC1

More guest stars on page 14 >>

On TARDIS:

POLICE PUBLIC CALL BOX

POLICE PUBLIC CALL BOX

POLICE TELEPHONE
FREE
FOR USE OF
PUBLIC
ADVICE & ASSISTANCE
OBTAINABLE IMMEDIATELY
OFFICER & CARS
RESPOND TO ALL CALLS
PULL TO OPEN

"They rounded Donna out from
being a shouting fishwife to someone
quite vulnerable and emotional"

CATHERINE TATE, *RT April 2008*

43

ERUPTION
Above: Donna had her fingers burnt in Pompeii.
Main picture: the guest stars of *The Fires of Pompeii*,
Peter Capaldi and Phil Davis, joined David Tennant and
Catherine Tate on the *RT* cover (2008)

MEMORABLE MOMENT
Donna is distraught that she and the Doctor were
instrumental in the eruption of Vesuvius. She pleads
with him – against his protests – to go back and
rescue "Just someone!" (*The Fires of Pompeii*, 2008)

HERE COMES THE BRIDE
Donna (Catherine Tate) was far from pleased to have
her wedding interrupted by the Doctor (David Tennant)
in *The Runaway Bride* (2006)

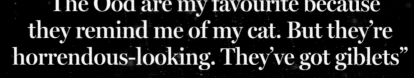

"The Ood are my favourite because they remind me of my cat. But they're horrendous-looking. They've got giblets"

CATHERINE TATE, *RT APRIL 2008*

OOD, GLORIOUS OOD
Tennant and Tate meet an Ood and Tim McInnerny (corrupt Mr Halpen) in *Planet of the Ood* and on the *RT* cover in 2008

GRACE HOLLOWAY
Daphne Ashbrook

Dates: 1996
Doctors: Sylvester McCoy, Paul McGann

Dr Grace Holloway made a one-off appearance in *Doctor Who: the Movie*, when the series was revived in a one-off film in 1996. An opera-loving cardiologist based in San Francisco, Grace operated on the wounded seventh Doctor and – unaware of his alien physiology – she triggered a regeneration. A recuperating and bewildered eighth Doctor requested her help in foiling the Master's plan to destroy Earth on Millennium Eve.

IN THEIR OWN WORDS

"I really had no idea that *Doctor Who* had such a huge and fanatical following. It wasn't until I heard Sylvester McCoy telling Paul [McGann] that he had no idea of what he was letting himself in for."
RT, May 1996

"I'm a 90s woman. What's really fun is that it's an equal relationship in many ways."
RT, May 1996

Paul McGann on the Doctor's first screen kiss: "It's not a licentious moment, though I know there have been stories that the Doctor has a steamy sex romp. Not true."
RT, March 1996

MEMORABLE MOMENT

The Doctor may have planted a paternal peck on some of his juvenile companions (Susan, Zoe) in the past, but Grace is the first person to receive a full-on lip-smacking kiss. For the Time Lord, it's an impulsive, mojo-discovering instant – not that Grace is complaining! "Good," she gasps. "Now do that again." And he obliges.
(Doctor Who: the Movie, 1996)

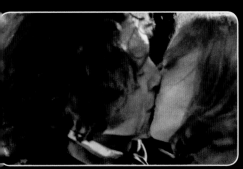

ENCORE
Would opera-loving Grace (Daphne Ashbrook) have enjoyed more Tardis adventures if the Paul McGann pilot had been more successful in the US?

IS THIS THE REAL HARRY?
Harry was kidnapped and duplicated by shape-shifting aliens under Loch Ness in *Terror of the Zygons* (1975)

HARRY SULLIVAN
Ian Marter

Dates: 1974–75 **Doctor:** Tom Baker

With his smart blazers and stiff upper lip, Surgeon Lieutenant Harry was resolutely old-school. Despite his mildly antagonistic relationship with fellow traveller Sarah Jane Smith, whom he called "old girl", he was extremely fond of her. And in his own slightly ham-fisted way, he defended the Doctor to the hilt, despite the latter once shouting, "Harry Sullivan is an imbecile!" After an intense bout of adventures involving the Time Lord's most iconic foes, Harry decided that British Rail was safer than the Tardis.

Ian Marter went on to write nine *Doctor Who* novels, and at one stage planned to co-write a *Who* feature film with Tom Baker. He died on his 42nd birthday in 1986.

In *The Sarah Jane Adventures* (2010), Sarah reminisced about her old pal (in the past tense): "Oh, I loved Harry. He was a doctor. He did such good work with vaccines. He saved thousands of lives."

IN THEIR OWN WORDS
The character of Harry was created before they quite knew how the fourth Doctor would work out. "They thought they might need someone to rush about and punch people on the nose occasionally if the Doctor couldn't. But when Tom Baker took over, it was obvious he didn't need that kind of help, so Harry turned into a slightly bumbling character who was as likely to mess things up as save the day – by accident."
RT, 20th Anniversary Special, 1983

MEMORABLE MOMENT
When the Doctor accidentally treads on a wobbly land mine and orders Harry to leave, Harry risks his life by rendering the device safe: "Don't you argue, Doctor! Now, just lift your foot... very, very gently."
(*Genesis of the Daleks*, 1975)

FEELING ANTSY
Ian (William Russell) and Susan (Carole Ann Ford) stumbled upon an enormous ant in *Planet of Giants*. Recorded in August 1964, it was one of the first episodes to come from BBC Television Centre. "Lime Grove Studio D had been very crushed," recalled Russell in 2010. "When we eventually moved into TV Centre, we were all amazed, because at last we had some space and could do things properly."

> "I said to (producer) Verity Lambert, 'So I'm the action man?' and she said, 'That's exactly right.' Bill Hartnell would play the leading role, but not be doing the fights. I was delighted. It was a very lovely job for me"
>
> WILLIAM RUSSELL, *RT November 2010*

IAN CHESTERTON
William Russell

Dates: 1963–65 **Doctor:** William Hartnell

In the early days of *Doctor Who*, with the original Doctor very much delineated as an anti-hero, it was down to Ian Chesterton to act as the show's moral compass and engage in any heroics. The task was well met by accomplished actor William Russell, who had already played Sir Lancelot, Nicholas Nickleby and Hamlet on TV.

A science teacher from 1960s London, Ian gamely struggled to keep pace with the Doctor's superior intellect. Good-natured and dapper, he could be relied upon for both brains and brawn, whether he was fighting Aztecs, Saracens or – on three occasions – the Daleks. In Ancient Rome, he was even called upon to row in a galley and train as a gladiator.

After two years aboard the erratic Tardis, Ian and his buddy Barbara returned to London in a Dalek timeship. That was 1965. Forty-five years later, in *The Sarah Jane Adventures*, it was revealed that Ian had married Barbara and they were still going strong as Cambridge professors.

MEMORABLE MOMENT
Palestine, 1191: Ian's heroic status is royally recognised when Richard the Lionheart (Julian Glover) dubs him Sir Ian, Knight of Jaffa. (*The Crusade*, 1965)

Riverside Studios, January 1965: *RT* followed the Doctor and Ian as they explored Vortis in *The Web Planet*. "I got on very well with Bill (Hartnell)," William Russell told *RT* in 2010. "I'd admired him so much as a film actor; he was terrifying in *Brighton Rock*. He had a quality I loved, which was that he was dangerous. It's a remarkable ability for an actor when suddenly they can turn and give you a shudder – a tingle down your spine."

IN THEIR OWN WORDS

On the first story: "We had to do a bit of filming at Ealing. The four of us were in a frivolous mood that day. We'd discovered we got along very well and had the same sense of humour. The scene was escaping from the prehistoric characters and running back to the Tardis. But we kept teasing the old BBC cameraman, who was trying to line us up. We were a bit naughty, I suppose."

On the Daleks: "At first we thought they were laughable. Mind you, we were introduced to them without their tops on. Just an actor sitting in this sort of bathtub base. When we started working with them, you could see how they'd become convincing. I had to pull out the creature inside. You don't actually see anything much in the episode, but it was a horrible thing – like an awful jellyfish." ***RT, November 2010***

AN UNEARTHLY CHAP

Time has not withered William Russell. Above, as Ian in 1963, and right, photographed at his north London home in 2010, reunited with the camera script to that very first episode, *An Unearthly Child*. "I did this, what is it, 47 years ago..? But I can still remember some of my lines!"

See extended interview at radiotimes.com/william-russell

RADIO TIMES February 11, 1965

3

Saturday

A new adventure begins on the Web Planet

DR. WHO

1 For Dr. Who and his companions the hazards of
5.40 their recent adventures among the Romans were
offset to some extent by the fact that they were
at least dealing with human antagonists—a
pleasant change after the Daleks. But at the end
of last week's story, Tardis had hardly dematerialised from
the Roman era before it became clear that things had gone
radically wrong and unearthly influences were at work again.
Observed the good Doctor: 'We seem to have been im-
prisoned by some kind of force. Something, somewhere, is
slowly plucking us down.'

But what—and where to? In the first episode of 'The Web
Planet' the time-travellers find themselves in eerie, sur-
roundings not unlike the surface of the moon; and when Dr.
Who attempts to take off again, the unknown force pre-
vents Tardis from moving. It is impossible to tell whether
a natural phenomenon is responsible, or some malevolent
intelligence. So when Vicki is affected by a strange noise
which only she can hear the Doctor and Ian set out to
explore, leaving Barbara and Vicki behind. Making a totally
unexpected discovery, and running into perils of a kind they
have never encountered before, they return to tell the others
—and get a most unpleasant shock.

Written by **Bill Strutton** and directed by **Richard Martin**,
who was also responsible for the second Dalek serial, this
latest story introduces some newcomers to the gallery of
denizens of outer space met by the crew of Tardis since they
first broke through the frontiers of time. For the Web Planet
is by no means as deserted as it seems. The visitors from
Earth are being closely watched . . .

"It was a desolate place – Vortis it was called. I can remember losing my tie in a pool of acid, and we had terrific problems with the butterflies (Menoptra). It was a marvellous idea, but it did rather drain the budget"

WILLIAM RUSSELL, *RT 40TH ANNIVERSARY SPECIAL, 2003*

CAPTAIN JACK HARKNESS
John Barrowman

Dates: from 2005
Doctors: Christopher Eccleston, David Tennant

A former time agent from the 51st century, Jack was posing as an RAF captain during the London Blitz and saved Rose from death as she fell from a barrage balloon. A charmer with a complex moral code, an outrageous flirt regardless of alien race or gender, Jack proved invaluable as a man of action alongside the more pacific Doctor.

He was exterminated by a Dalek but revived by Rose using the power of the time vortex – an action that rendered him immortal and set him up for his spin-off series, *Torchwood*. Jack returned to help the Doctor and Martha fight the Master, when it was hinted that he might one day become the Face of Boe.

We last saw Jack drowning his sorrows in a space-age bar – until the Doctor fixed him up with Alonso (Russell Tovey), a survivor of the starship *Titanic*.

CAPTAIN FANTASTIC
The indestructible Jack bolstered the Doctor's bid to thwart the Master in *Last of the Time Lords* (2007)

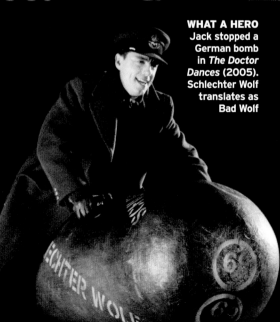

WHAT A HERO
Jack stopped a German bomb in *The Doctor Dances* (2005). Schlechter Wolf translates as Bad Wolf

IN THEIR OWN WORDS

"I was always an assistant. I'm not kidding! When I was told I'd got the *Doctor Who* job, I was walking through Covent Garden with my niece, and I literally screamed and jumped around because I was so excited."
RT, May 2005

"Chris [Eccleston] had this thing he used to say: 'Line fear.' The first day I heard it, I said, 'What's that?' He said, 'You'll know.' I didn't understand until three days in, when I read the script and I had paragraph upon paragraph of stuff to say. Line fear!"
RT, May 2005

On returning to *Doctor Who*: "It's not the Captain Jack from *Torchwood*. He's not angsty or moody. Captain Jack from *Doctor Who* is a little more light-hearted, because he's back where he wants to be. One of his main objectives over the past couple of years is to figure out why Jack is the way he is. Now he can let the Doctor take responsibility for everything."
RT, June 2007

MEMORABLE MOMENT

When Jack hears the Tardis landing to refuel outside Torchwood HQ, he's so determined to rejoin the Doctor that he jumps through the air and clings to the police box exterior. It dematerialises and takes him along into the space/time continuum... (*Utopia*, 2007)

FRONT TO JACK
As the handsome star of *Torchwood*, John Barrowman made the cover of *Radio Times* in October 2006 (bottom) and July 2009 (below)

SHAZIA MIRZA ★ FRANKIE BOYLE ★ CHARLIE BROOKER

radiotimes.com
4–10 July 2009 £1.10

RadioTimes

Gerry
Robinson
How to spot
a business
in trouble

Shane
Warne
The Ashes?
"I'll be getting
itchy feet..."

Torchwood

Five episodes... five nights...
and one great big explosive story
Torchwood: Children of Earth, Monday–Friday BBC1, BBC HD

AND IT ALL STARTS HERE... ≫

www.radiotimes.com

RadioTimes

21–27 OCTOBER 2006 98p

EXCLUSIVE
CAPTAIN
JACK
IS BACK!
The story behind *Torchwood*:
the new sci-fi crime thriller from
the makers of *Doctor Who*
Sunday BBC3 / Wednesday BBC2

"It's not the Captain Jack from *Torchwood*.
He's not angsty or moody"

JOHN BARROWMAN, *RT* JUNE 2007

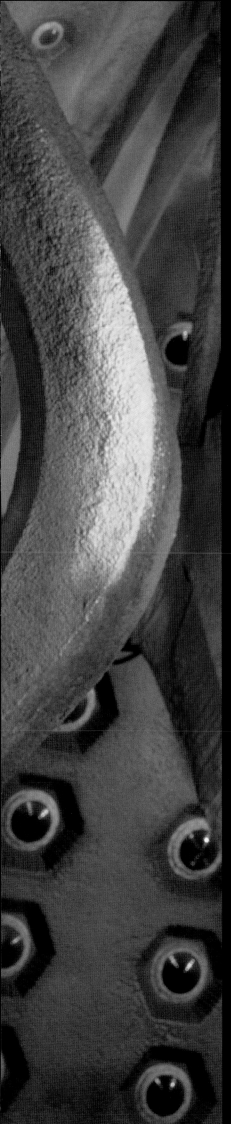

LIFE-CHANGING EVENTS
Above: Rose and Jackie tend to the newly regenerated Doctor in *The Christmas Invasion* (2005)
Below: Jackie meets parallel-world Pete (Shaun Dingwall) in *Doomsday* (2006)

JACKIE TYLER
Camille Coduri

Dates: 2005–2010
Doctors: Christopher Eccleston, David Tennant

Jackie was – extraordinarily – the first "companion mother" seen in *Doctor Who*. Lubricious but adorable, she was fiercely protective of Rose and, after the death of husband Pete, lived her life through their daughter. Jackie distrusted the Doctor, once slapping his chops for absconding with Rose. She also fancied him rotten. She was eventually united with another Pete from a parallel Earth and decided to live there with him.

IN THEIR OWN WORDS

"I love Jackie. She's very passionate and dramatic. She's so annoying. She's a lazy woman and likes to live through her daughter. Rose is her world – but then Rose lost her father when she was a baby, so their relationship is a big thing."
RT, March 2005

"I'm very proud of her because she restrains herself from becoming a complete floozy. Instead she becomes very nurturing. There's a side to her you've not seen before – she's less selfish, amazingly so. Because she's quite self-centred really. And the Doctor has changed. She'd just got used to the other one, and suddenly... She really fancies this one as well. A lot! I think both Rose and Jackie are in love with this wonderful man. He's gorgeous and divine!"
RT, December 2005

MEMORABLE MOMENT

Jackie revises her opinion of the Doctor after Rose reveals he took her back to see Pete on the day he died. To help get the Tardis working again, Jackie turns up outside the police box with a pick-up truck. "Rodrigo – he owes me a favour, and never mind why." (*The Parting of the Ways*, 2005)

JACKSON LAKE
David Morrissey

Dates: 2008 **Doctor:** David Tennant

Poor deluded Jackson – only tenuously a companion and certainly not a Doctor, as he believed himself to be in the 2008 Christmas special, *The Next Doctor*. There's no denying that he cut a swaggering Time Lordly figure in his silk tie and frock coat, bravely defending Victorian London from Cybershades. He even had his own companion, Rosita. But the tenth Doctor established that this "next Doctor" was in fact Jackson Lake, formerly a teacher whose wife had been killed and whose son had been abducted.

In a "fugue state" of bereavement, his mind had absorbed data about the real Doctor from an "infostamp" belonging to the Cybermen. As they joined forces to avert the Cyber menace, the Time Lord set Jackson on the road to recovery.

IN THEIR OWN WORDS

"They've asked me to do stuff before but because of other commitments I was unable to. Then this came along: the Christmas special, which has added kudos and an amazing character. The ultimate character, really. But a terribly tragic character, too. Something terrible has happened to him... The Doctors become great friends. In this episode, the Doctor [David Tennant] doesn't have a companion, which is rare, and my Doctor fills that gap."
RT, December 2008

Russell T Davies: "Anyone playing the Doctor has to be capable of anything – action, heartbreak, comedy, wielding a sonic screwdriver – and David Morrissey's got that in spades. He's one of those actors who can turns on a sixpence: light-hearted one minute, tragic the next."
RT, December 2008

MEMORABLE MOMENT

Answering a cry for help, the Doctor is gobsmacked when a complete stranger turns up on the scene and declares, "I'm the Doctor. Simply the Doctor. The one, the only and the best." He even produces a sonic screwdriver and parrots his catchphrase "*Allons-y!*" (*The Next Doctor*, 2008)

"In this episode, the Doctor doesn't have a companion, which is rare, and my Doctor fills that gap"

DAVID MORRISSEY, *RT DECEMBER 2008*

YOUR LISTINGS FOR 6–12 DECEMBER

www.radiotimes.com

6–12 DECEMBER 2008 £1.05

RadioTimes

IT'S RT'S
REVIEW OF
THE YEAR!
with Stephen Fry,
Catherine Tate,
Gareth Malone,
Andrew Marr,
Harry Hill
& many more!
See page 16

PLUS
Richard
Armitage
Jack Dee
The Hairy
Bakers

ONLY IN RT

WHO'S THE DOCTOR?

Don't miss our exclusive preview of
David Morrissey and **David Tennant**
in the *Doctor Who* Christmas special!

OPEN THE COVER TO FIND OUT WHO THEY'RE UP AGAINST ▶▶▶

Meet Dervla Kirwan as
Miss Hartigan
(with her knights in shining armour)

WHAT FRIENDS ARE FOR

For our 6 December 2008 gatefold cover, *RT* photographed Davids Morrissey and Tennant (main picture and above) in Wales and added the wintry backdrop afterwards. As "the next Doctor" Jackson Lake, Morrissey had his own companion – Rosita (Velile Tshabalala, left). The villainess of the piece (above) was Miss Hartigan (Dervla Kirwan)

> "It was wonderful playing a period character who'd never seen a car or a TV set, being transported into the future"
>
> FRAZER HINES, *RT 1983*

MEMORABLE MOMENT

The comedy-duo partnership of the Doctor and Jamie is shown clearly when the Doctor, realising he's holding Jamie's hand instead of Victoria's, flings it aside in Oliver Hardy-style annoyance.

JAMIE McCRIMMON
Frazer Hines

Dates: 1966–69, 1983, 1985
Doctors: Patrick Troughton, Colin Baker

The 18th-century Scottish piper is a popular entry in the sidekicks' roll of honour. Courageous, kilt-wearing Jamie (James Robert McCrimmon) could adapt to any time and situation by translating them into terms that he could comprehend. He really came into his own after Ben and Polly's departure from the series, and was protective of the Doctor, Zoe and especially Victoria.

From the Battle of Culloden to the planet of *The War Games*, Jamie was always ready to take on redcoats, Daleks, Yeti, Cybermen and other "beasties" with bravado and his Gaelic battle cry, "Creag an tuire!" He only fell out with the Doctor seriously once when the Doctor put him through a test to find the "human factor" in *The Evil of the Daleks*. But at least it brought Victoria into their lives, whom Jamie was rather sweet on.

One of the longest-running male companions, he was returned to his Highland home by the Time Lords when they put the Doctor on trial, although he reappeared briefly in *The Five Doctors* (1983) and at length in *The Two Doctors* (1985).

MAGICAL MYSTERY TOUR
Frazer Hines (above) with co-stars Patrick Troughton and Deborah Watling (Victoria) on the BBC location coach in September 1967. Snowdonia was masquerading as Tibet, 1935, for the filming of *The Abominable Snowmen*. Hines (right) tended to cover up between takes: "It's no joke on a windy day"

"Wearing a kilt could be a bit chilly at times, but the big question people always wanted to know was: did I or didn't I wear anything underneath it?"

FRAZER HINES, *RT 10TH ANNIVERSARY SPECIAL 1973*

IN THEIR OWN WORDS

"I always thought the phrase 'blue with cold' was a figure of speech but filming in Margate the other day my knees did literally turn blue... I'd love to be a comedian. I often see bits of *Doctor Who* scripts as a sort of Morecambe and Wise double act. Imagine me going up to Patrick Troughton, putting my arm around him and saying, 'My little short fat hairy friend...' "
RT, February 1968

On wearing a kilt: "It's no joke on a windy day. And have you ever tried riding a horse in one?"
RT, April 1969

"I'm not really a science fiction man. I didn't even watch the Moon landings. But then, as I told people, I'd already been there in *Doctor Who*. I always like costume parts, where I can use an accent, so Jamie was just right for me. He was a refugee from the Battle of Culloden, and originally had a real Highlands accent, but I eventually mellowed it to a sort of 'TV Scots'. I don't have an accent myself, though my mother is a Scot.

   "Wearing a kilt could be a bit chilly at times, but the big question people always wanted to know was: did I or didn't I wear anything underneath it? Well, I'll tell you. I did. Usually football shorts so I could get a game of soccer as soon as I'd finished on set."
RT, 10th Anniversary Special, 1973

"It was wonderful playing a period character who'd never seen a car or a TV set, being transported into the future, which probably explains why Jamie looked bewildered most of the time... Mine were once voted the Sexiest Legs on Television in a viewers' poll and, if I remember right, Keith Barron came second and Liza Goddard third."
RT, 20th Anniversary Special, 1983

CANNY COMPANION
Above: a rare colour shot from *The Mind Robber* (1968) Main picture opposite: Frazer Hines and Deborah Watling (who played Victoria) were reunited with a Yeti in 1973 for *RT's 10th Anniversary Special*

FACE SWAP
Jamie was played briefly by Hamish Wilson in *The Mind Robber* when Hines was off work with chicken pox – the Doctor mixed up his face in the Land of Fiction

JO GRANT
Katy Manning

Dates: 1971–74, 2010
Doctors: Jon Pertwee, Matt Smith

Often wearing thigh boots, miniskirts and rings on every finger, ditsy but utterly beguiling, Jo (Josephine) Grant claimed to be a fully trained secret agent with expertise in cryptology, safe-breaking and explosives. With a leg-up from her uncle at the UN, she secured a post at Unit, and the third Doctor was dismayed when the Brigadier offloaded Jo on him. "I'll have a properly qualified assistant or none at all!" he blazed.

However, the pair quickly became inseparable. The Doctor formed a closer bond with Jo than anyone else since the departure of his granddaughter, Susan. Jo was immensely popular with the public and, at the time, became the longest-running female companion with three years under her belt. The Doctor could barely disguise his heartbreak when she left him to go up the Amazon with a fungus-growing ecologist,

Professor Clifford Jones – "a sort of younger you".

After a 37-year break, and years living in Australia, Katy Manning reprised her character in *The Sarah Jane Adventures* (2010). Now Jo Jones, a mother of seven and with 12 grandchildren, she'd spent her life travelling the world as an environmental protestor.

"Sometimes I think I've never stopped running," she said, moved to catch up with her old friend, the Doctor – albeit in his 11th persona. Of course, Jo was familiar with face-changing Time Lords after *The Three Doctors* (1972–73).

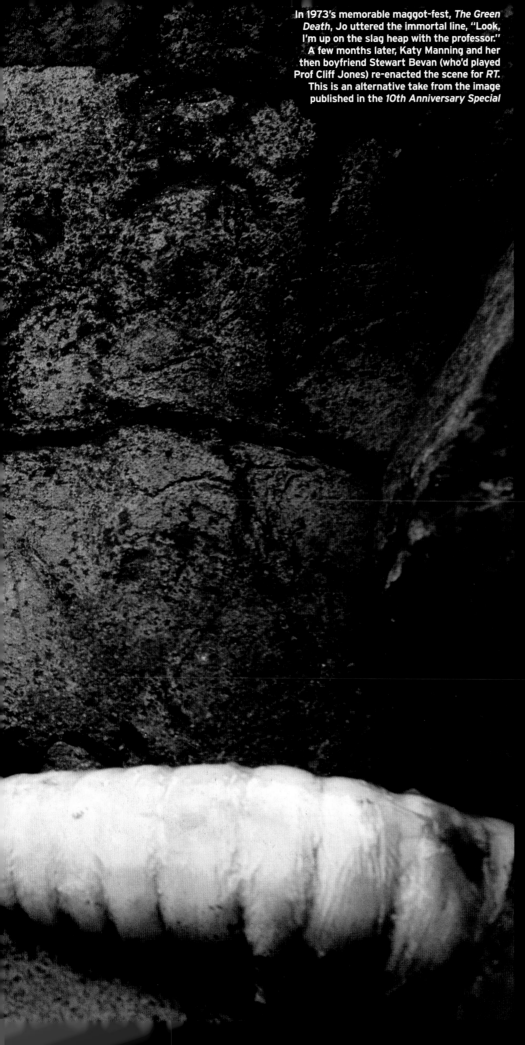

In 1973's memorable maggot-fest, *The Green Death*, Jo uttered the immortal line, "Look, I'm up on the slag heap with the professor." A few months later, Katy Manning and her then boyfriend Stewart Bevan (who'd played Prof Cliff Jones) re-enacted the scene for *RT*. This is an alternative take from the image published in the *10th Anniversary Special*

"I'm supposed to crack safes and pick locks, *Avengers*-style, but I really need looking after. I'm always in a muddle myself, but Jon [Pertwee] is so stable and marvellous. He's forever picking up my scripts or whatever it is I've left behind. I'm as blind as a bat without my glasses and fall over a lot. Filming *Terror of the Autons* in Dunstable, I had to run across a heap of rubble. I fell flat on my face and twisted my ankle."
RT, May 1971

On *Who*: "The groovy thing about it is that it's lunatic and completely nutty. I am myself as Jo, I suppose. Jo's a scatty, slightly messy, very happy person. And that's me."
RT, January 1972

"I first met Jon Pertwee in the foyer of TV Centre months before I started *Doctor Who* and he thought I was a bit of all right. When I went for an audition I was just one of a crowd, but I screamed and freaked out and got the job... There were some not so funny moments. I once had to drive a hovercraft, but pushed the wrong button. One side deflated and 40 sailors fell on top of me. It might have been fun for them..."
RT, 10th Anniversary Special, 1973

"I couldn't believe it when I was offered the part. At first I was so nervous, I learned everybody else's lines as well as my own. Perhaps I was lucky enough to be on when *Doctor Who's* impact was at its greatest, and that's why I'm so well remembered. As Jo, I had no super brains and was very ordinary and a little bit dim. I loved the series. I loved the people and I didn't want to leave. But it was time for a new type of girl."
RT, September 1978

MEMORABLE MOMENT
Azal, a fearsome 30ft-tall Dæmon, is about to vaporise the Doctor, but loyal Jo instinctively thrusts herself into the deadly ray. "No, he's a good man. Kill me, not him!" Now that's devotion! (*The Dæmons*, 1971)

"When I went for an audition I was just one of a crowd, but I screamed and freaked out and got the job"

KATY MANNING, *RT 1973*

THAT 70S LOOK
Above: "Princess Josephine of Tardis" conferred with the hermaphrodite hexapod Alpha Centauri and the Martian Lord Izlyr in *The Curse of Peladon* (1972)

Below: Katy Manning photographed at home in Chiswick for *RT*, January 1972

FUN GUY
"Of all the silly young goats... You'll contaminate my spores."
Clumsy Jo (Katy Manning) and her future husband Cliff Jones
(Stewart Bevan) got off on the wrong foot in *The Green Death* (1973)

MASTERFUL PAIRING
"Thank you, Miss Grant. We'll let you know."
The original Master (Roger Delgado) was not
fooled — for long — by Jo's play-acting in
Frontier in Space (1973). Both refreshing
characters had been introduced to *Doctor
Who* (and on the *RT* cover) in January 1971

ANOTHER DIMENSION
Above: the Doctor (Jon Pertwee) took Jo (Katy Manning) on her first Tardis trip in *Colony in Space*. This unusual *RT* shot, from March 1971, shows the rear view of the Tardis doors – with weights below to prevent any set-wobbling – and the view beyond into Studio 4 at BBC Television Centre

***RT* LETTERS**
In July 1973, *Doctor Who* producer Barry Letts eased the handover between Jo and Sarah – two classic companions he had devised

Come back, Katy Manning

Why is it that when you accept and love someone who is on TV every week she suddenly leaves the series in which she has been so fantastic? I am talking about dear Katy Manning, playing Jo Grant in *Dr Who* (BBC1), of course.

I've always watched the programme from the William Hartnell days. Now I am 21, and in the last episode of the recent series when Jo told the Doctor she was leaving him to get married, I could not help myself – I just cried. Jon Pertwee acted just as hurt as I felt when he walked out of the house and drove away.

(Miss) B. A. Lovett
Hornchurch

BARRY LETTS, Producer, 'Dr Who,' replies:
I'm just as sad as anybody that Katy's leaving the series, but we must remember that she has been playing Jo Grant for three years. Even as gilded a cage as a long-running series can become too confining; Katy naturally wants to spread her wings a bit.

Sarah Jane Smith, who joins the Doctor next season, is a very different person from Jo Grant, but I am quite sure that Elisabeth Sladen, who is to play her, will become just as popular, and indeed just as loved, as Katy has been.

"It's groovy granny time. I used to lift Jo's voice right up, but there was a moment on set when I forgot that Jo is 40 years older"

KATY MANNING,
RT OCTOBER 2010

PURE KATY

Above: in her debut story *Terror of the Autons* (1971) and an *RT* cartoon by Frank Bellamy

Main picture: returning to the Tardis after 37 years for *The Sarah Jane Adventures* in 2010

Bottom! She caused a minor furore in 1978 when she posed nude with a Dalek for *Girl Illustrated*

K•9

Voiced by John Leeson and David Brierley

Dates: 1977–81, 1983, from 2006
Doctors: Tom Baker, David Tennant

A robotic dog from the year 5000 – created and donated to the Doctor by Professor Marius – K•9 was originally devised by writers Bob Baker and Dave Martin and intended for one story, *The Invisible Enemy*, but producer Graham Williams immediately saw further potential. The original prop was designed by Tony Harding and built by the BBC's Visual Effects Department.

K•9's nose-mounted laser and vast knowledge proved invaluable on many occasions, and when the first model stayed behind on Gallifrey to look after Leela, the Doctor unveiled a Mark II! That K•9 eventually remained in E-Space with Romana, and the Doctor subsequently bequeathed two other models to his old friend, Sarah Jane Smith.

His wagging aerial-tale and rotating scanner-ears made him a big hit with children. So much so that he returned to the revived series in 2006 and featured in *The Sarah Jane Adventures*, and starred in both the one-off drama *K•9 and Company* (1981) and his very own series, the recent British/Australian co-production *K•9*.

K•9's distinctive clipped voice has always been provided by actor John Leeson, apart from during the 17th season (1979–80) when David Brierley gave him a peculiarly prissy air.

IN THEIR OWN WORDS

John Leeson: "In the early days, K•9's radio control apparatus was on the same wavelength as the cameras, so when he got too close to them, he'd go berserk, charging all over the place. I felt terrible and was sure that everybody blamed me."
RT, 20th Anniversary Special, 1983

John Leeson: "During rehearsals, I actually scrabbled around the floor on all fours to give the other actors something to react to. But in the studio, the radio-controlled prop was used and I sat in my little booth."
RT, May 1996

David Brierley: "In *The Horns of Nimon*, K•9 was very important. So important it seemed that Tom Baker was heard to mutter that the show ought to be renamed *Doctor Bloody K•9*. He didn't mean it."
RT, May 1996

Tom Baker: "When we had visitors on set, John Leeson would be in the scanner wagon to do the voice of K•9, and I'd be outside doing a crossword with the dog next to me and he'd say, 'Do you need some help, Master?' There are out-takes that they can't possibly show of me kicking K•9 and telling him to f*** off. I'm just an old comic really."
RT, 40th Anniversary Special, 2003

MEMORABLE MOMENT

K•9's reply to the Doctor's criticism of computer limitations is to beat him at chess: "Machine mind computes mate in six moves!"
(*The Sun Makers*, 1977)

IT'S A DOG'S LIFE

K•9 in the 2006 *Doctor Who* story *School Reunion* (top), in which the robotic hound was paired once again with Elisabeth Sladen (right) following 1981's *K•9 and Company* (above).

KAMELION
Voiced by Gerald Flood

Dates: 1983–84
Doctor: Peter Davison

Not the cleverest idea the show has ever come up with, Kamelion was a partially sentient shape-changing robot discovered by the Master on the planet Xeriphas. He joined the Doctor after being freed from the Master's control, but knowing he was vulnerable to manipulation, he preferred to stay in the Tardis. This meant Kamelion remained unseen between his introduction in *The King's Demons* and his termination at the Doctor's hands six stories later in *Planet of Fire*. His "shyness" was written in when the prop that was used for his on-screen realisation continually malfunctioned.

At least Kamelion was unusual. During his brief stint he took the form of John of England (also played by Kamelion's voice artist, Gerald Flood), Tegan (Janet Fielding), Peri's stepfather Howard (Dallas Adams), the Doctor (Peter Davison) and the Master (Anthony Ainley).

MEMORABLE MOMENT
His destruction (probably celebrated by cast and crew)! (*Planet of Fire*, 1984)

CYBER-KING
The lute-strumming Kamelion in *The King's Demons* (1983) and one of his alter egos, King John (played by Gerald Flood, who also provided the robot's voice)

DAUGHTER OF THE GODS
Trojan handmaiden Katarina (Adrienne Hill) appeared in just five episodes before her sudden demise in the mid-60s epic *The Daleks' Master Plan*

KATARINA
Adrienne Hill

Dates: 1965
Doctor: William Hartnell

Katarina was a demure, softly spoken Trojan handmaiden. Her mistress Cassandra had prophesied her death, so she fully believed that the Doctor was a great god taking her on a "journey through the beyond" to "the place of perfection" in his temple, the Tardis. After just five episodes, she made a shocking early exit from the series (see below).

In the mid-1980s, long after she'd stopped acting, Adrienne Hill was invited to *Doctor Who* conventions, delighted and surprised to be celebrated as a fully fledged companion and for what was, in effect, five weeks' work 20 years earlier. She died in 1997.

IN THEIR OWN WORDS

Adrienne Hill became a drama teacher in south London. "There was an item on BBC *Breakfast Time* a few weeks ago about the new female companion, in which they showed pictures of all the old ones. One of my pupils recognised me, which was very nice because before that I don't think they really believed I'd ever actually been an actress."
RT, 20th Anniversary Special, 1983

MEMORABLE MOMENT

Katarina is the first companion in the series to die. The Doctor's mission against the Daleks is hindered when a desperate convict holds her hostage in a spaceship airlock. Struggling free, Katarina opens the ship's outer door, ejecting herself and the convict to a silent death in space. (*The Daleks' Master Plan*, 1965)

LEELA
Louise Jameson

Dates: 1977–78
Doctor: Tom Baker

If there's one companion who fully deserves the description "brave", it's Leela. This fearless warrior of the Sevateem saved the Doctor's neck on countless occasions, although it took some time for his "Don't kill" instruction to sink in. An instinct-driven savage, armed with a knife and lethal Janis thorns, the bronzed, animal-skin-wearing Leela liked nothing more than a good scrap – which made her docile departure when she fell in love with a Gallifreyan guard all the more uncharacteristic, not to say laughable.

MEMORABLE MOMENT
Captured and about to be killed by a disfigured 51st-century despot, Leela delivers one of her juiciest curses: "When we are both in the great hereafter, I shall hunt you down, Bent Face, and put you through my agony a thousand times!"
(*The Talons of Weng-Chiang*, 1977)

"I based Leela on two characters I knew well – Bosi my dog and the little girl upstairs, making a half-child, half-animal. Though I had to have a lot of make-up for the part, I'm recognised everywhere. When kids ask for my autograph, they say, 'Put your real name in. Write Leela.'"
RT, September 1978

"I got a huge amount of fan mail from children. My favourite was from a four-year-old boy who wrote, 'Leela, why don't you put some clothes on?'"
RT, 20th Anniversary Special, 1983

"I was delighted to become Leela because *Doctor Who* had been a Saturday ritual, with baked beans in front of the fire, for my family since it started. I remember thinking I could now afford to build some shelves. I must have been very naive. It didn't occur to me that running around in that revealing costume would have that effect on male viewers."
RT, November 1988

"I think Leela should have died heroically, saving the Doctor. She was that kind of savage really, always seeking the glorious route out, never the romantic one. Instead she married some poor guard on Gallifrey, which was, frankly, stupid and illogical."
RT, May 1996

PUTTING ON THE WAR PAINT
Once Jameson was cast as Leela, the make-up artists experimented with a darker shade for her skin – visible in these early photos – but this was made lighter to produce the warrior's final look

"I was astounded that I became a sex symbol. But I suppose if you put somebody in leathers and bang them on after the football results, it's inevitable"

LOUISE JAMESON, *RT NOVEMBER 1993*

LIZ SHAW
Caroline John

Dates: 1970, 1983
Doctor: Jon Pertwee

Professor Elizabeth Shaw was recruited to Unit, against her will, by the Brigadier. "I have an important research programme going ahead at Cambridge," she bristled. An expert in meteorites, with degrees in medicine and physics, Liz was just the all-rounder he needed in the fight against alien invaders. No-nonsense and frosty, she warmed to Unit's scientific adviser, the third Doctor, but became fed up working as his assistant, passing test tubes. Liz survived four stories (undergoing several makeovers and changes of hairstyle and wigs) before returning to Cambridge.

She made a cameo appearance in *The Five Doctors* (1983), then in *The Sarah Jane Adventures* (2010) it was mentioned in passing that Liz was stationed on a Moonbase, presumably working once more for Unit.

IN THEIR OWN WORDS

'It's a good, well-written part. And though most of my work has been in the theatre, I'm really looking forward to this television season."
RT, September 1969

'Liz Shaw was a miniskirted lady – with a first-class brain, mind you. I bought an encyclopaedia to look up half the things she was talking about. I joined at the same time as Jon Pertwee, which was lovely because the programme was getting a new sense of purpose and being taken rather more seriously."
RT, 10th Anniversary Special, 1973

'I was excited at first to be a brainy girl, but all the directors wanted really was a sexy piece. It wasn't very realistic, looking back. I wasn't allowed trousers [*RT* let her in 1973, right] and it was such an effort looking glamorous on cold clay-pits and rubbish dumps. I enjoyed the series but found it restricting after a while."
RT, September 1978

PRIMED FOR ACTION
Spearhead from Space (1970) was a first for *Doctor Who*, and not just for Caroline John as Liz Shaw: it was the first story for Jon Pertwee as the third Doctor and the first to be produced in colour!

VINTAGE BESSIE
Nicholas Courtney and Caroline John were reunited by *RT* in 1973. The Doctor named his old-fashioned yellow motor car "Bessie" – another diminutive name for Elizabeth – in his second adventure with Liz

"I was excited at first to be a brainy girl, but all the directors wanted really was a sexy piece"

CAROLINE JOHN, *RT SEPTEMBER 1978*

MEMORABLE MOMENT
On a parallel, *1984*-like world, an alternate Liz has become a cold-hearted soldier. The Doctor divines that Section Leader Elizabeth Shaw once hoped to be a scientist just like her counterpart, and she starts to thaw towards him. (*Inferno*, 1970)

TIME FOR A CHANGE
Although *Inferno* allowed Liz to have an alter ego, it was Caroline John's last full story – she was pregnant at the time

MARTHA JONES
Freema Agyeman

Dates: 2007–2010
Doctor: David Tennant

Spirited young medical student Martha became entangled with the Doctor when her hospital was transported to the Moon by the Judoon. Over subsequent encounters with William Shakespeare in Elizabethan London, the Daleks in Depression-era New York, and posing as a maid in an English public school in 1913, Martha became romantically attached to the Time Lord.

When her feelings went unreciprocated, she left the Doctor, who later found her recruited to Unit and Torchwood (she appeared in three episodes of the spin-off series in 2008), married to Mickey Smith and working as a freelance alien hunter.

MEMORABLE MOMENT

With the Doctor and Earth's population enslaved by the Master, it's up to Martha to save the world. Typically self-effacing, she says, "If Martha Jones became a legend then that's wrong, because my name isn't important. There's someone else. The man who sent me out there, the man who told me to walk the Earth. And his name is the Doctor." (*Last of the Time Lords*, 2007)

WHAT'S IN A KISS?
Not long after they met, the Doctor (David Tennant) locked lips with Martha (Freema Agyeman), but only to give her a genetic transfer. She returned the kiss later to save his life, and on their travels together she fell for him – big time!

KEEPING UP WITH THE JONESES
In *The Lazarus Experiment* (2007), the Doctor got a mixed reception from Martha's family – sister Tish (Gugu Mbatha-Raw), mum Francine (Adjoa Andoh) and brother Leo (Reggie Yates), who became semi-regular characters

"Martha's grounded and happy with where she's at, then the Doctor comes along and blows everything out of the water for her"

FREEMA AGYEMAN, *RT MARCH 2007*

BOX

GIRL POWER
Freema Agyeman and Billie Piper were photographed together in Cardiff for *RT*'s cover and feature about "The Doctor's Women" in June 2008. Rose and Martha joined forces with Donna and other companions to help defeat the Daleks in 2008's series-four finale

"Martha is very different from Rose. She's academic and independent, has her own flat and she's almost qualified to be a doctor"

FREEMA AGYEMAN, *RT MARCH 2007*

OLD FATHER TIME
In *Last of the Time Lords* (2007), the Doctor, aged via genetic manipulation by his deadly enemy the Master, whispered an instruction in Martha's ear...

IN THEIR OWN WORDS

"Martha is very different from Rose. She's academic and independent, has her own flat and she's almost qualified to be a doctor. She's grounded and happy with where she's at, then the Doctor comes along and blows everything out of the water for her. Martha has an old head on young shoulders and that's what makes her more challenging of the Doctor. She wants answers."
RT, March 2007

Russell T Davies: "She's 23, a medical student, and her family's going into meltdown. Martha's stuck in the middle as a peacemaker. Just the sort of woman who needs an escape. She's thrown straight in at the deep end, away from Earth, surrounded by aliens and struggling to save the lives of everyone around her."
RT, March 2007

"Where do you go after you've saved the world and confessed your love to the Doctor, who hasn't returned the feelings? She encounters the Doctor again, but it's in a more professional capacity."
RT, February 2008

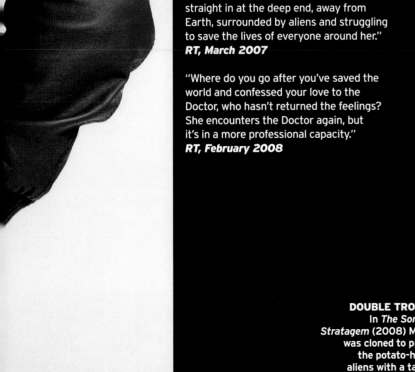

DOUBLE TROUBLE
In *The Sontaran Stratagem* (2008) Martha was cloned to provide the potato-headed aliens with a tactical advantage against Unit

"Where do you go after you've confessed your love to the Doctor, who hasn't returned the feelings?"

FREEMA AGYEMAN, *RT FEBRUARY 2008*

HOW TO SAVE THE WORLD
Above: Freema Agyeman in a behind-the-scenes shot from *Journey's End* (2008)

Below: Agyeman with David Tennant accepting their framed gift at the 2008 *Radio Times* Covers Party

WHO FOR THE PRICE OF ONE
Freema Agyeman's first appearance in *Doctor Who* was in *Army of Ghosts* (2006) as Adeola Oshodi, a Torchwood One technician who was killed by the Cybermen. Martha later told the Doctor that Adeola was her cousin.

MEL
Bonnie Langford

Dates: 1986–87
Doctors: Colin Baker, Sylvester McCoy

Mel (or Melanie) was a computer programmer from Pease Pottage, prone to panto-large exuberance and piercing shrieks, and determined to help the Doctor shape up on a diet of orange juice. Viewers never actually saw how the pair first met. Mel was a companion from the sixth Doctor's future, revealed during his trial by the Time Lords, but paradoxically she left with him in his own present at the end of the trial. Confused..?

Mel went on to have a riot with the seventh Doctor, but they parted company on Iceworld when she chose to keep an eye on space vagabond Glitz. Mel left the Doctor in the capable hands of their new chum, Ace.

ROCK CHICK
Bonnie Langford filming *Time and the Rani* with Mark Greenstreet (as colourful Lakertyan, Ikona) in a Somerset quarry in April 1987

IN THEIR OWN WORDS

"Melanie is a bit headstrong and nosey, so although she recognises the Doctor is the leader, she helps out by running off and investigating things for herself. [Mel's first episode] is set in the Doctor's future. You never learn how I got to travel with him.

"I'd like to break away from the kind of work people expect me to do... *Doctor Who* is a very happy series to work on, and we had lots of wonderful guest stars like Honor Blackman, Lynda Bellingham and Michael Jayston."
RT, November 1986

> "I thought after a while that people might get a bit fed up with this red-haired loon running around shouting 'Doctor!' and so I left"
>
> BONNIE LANGFORD, *RT May 1996*

MAKING A SPLASH
Mel (Bonnie Langford) and seventh Doctor Sylvester McCoy fend off a robotic crab in a pool in the forbidding *Paradise Towers* (1987)

MEMORABLE MOMENT

The Rani (a wicked Time Lady) has disguised herself as Mel to bamboozle the newly regenerated seventh Doctor. Kate O'Mara as Bonnie Langford? Bizarre barely covers it. (*Time and the Rani*, 1987)

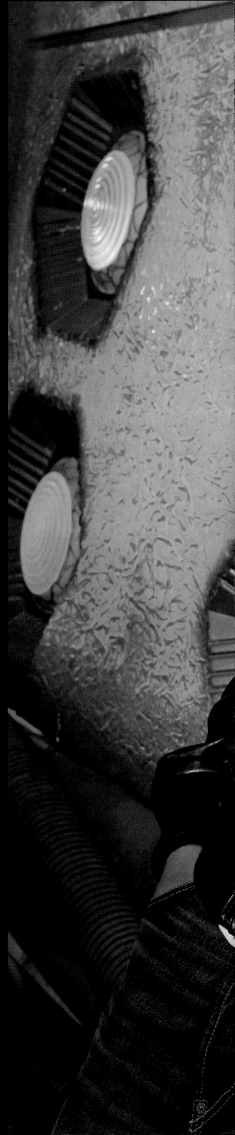

MICKEY SMITH
Noel Clarke

Dates: 2005–2010
Doctors: Christopher Eccleston, David Tennant

Mickey began as Rose's terrified boyfriend and ended up as Martha Jones's courageous, Earth-defending husband! He was initially jealous of the Doctor and his friendship with Rose, and in return the Doctor teased him by getting his name wrong or calling him "Mickey the Idiot". He later called himself "tin dog" after likening his function as a companion to that of K•9 Mark III, but the Doctor, impressed by Mickey's growing initiative, allowed him to travel in the Tardis.

A crack in the time vortex sent Mickey into a parallel world, where he met his doppelgänger, Ricky. After Ricky was killed by Cybermen, Mickey stayed behind to look after his grandmother (who had died in the real world).

During separate adventures in the real world, Mickey helped in the Battle of Canary Wharf against both the Cybermen and Daleks, and joined the Doctor's army of companions to defeat the Daleks' Earth-hijack plot. Thereafter, he never went back to the parallel realm.

The last time we saw Mickey, he was married to Martha. The pair had become freelance alien fighters and were battling a Sontaran.

THE HAND OF FEAR
Above: in *Doomsday* (2006), Mickey (Noel Clarke) touched the Genesis Ark, accidentally activating a prison ship containing myriad Daleks

MEMORABLE MOMENT
Fleeing the Cybermen, Mickey finds reserves of courage and comes to the Doctor and Rose's rescue. Then Rose asks him how he learnt to fly a zeppelin, Mickey replies: "PlayStation!" (*The Age of Steel*, 2006)

"Mickey's a coward, a sort of Shaggy from *Scooby-Doo*. He provides comic relief – he becomes the damsel in distress"

NOEL CLARKE, *RT MARCH 2005*

IN THEIR OWN WORDS

"I went to a *Doctor Who* convention and people
were going, 'He's a bit of a weed, isn't he? When's
he going to get braver?' The answer, happily, is:
round about now [*The Christmas Invasion*]. When
Jackie's Christmas tree comes to life, it's Mickey
who's up there playing the hero. He was getting
unpopular as he was so cowardly, but I have
a sneaking suspicion that will all change.
I seriously think he's going to be very popular
by the end of all this."
RT, December 2005

Russell T Davies: "Mickey's has been one of the
longest and most complicated stories. He starts out
as a complete coward, an idiot, a boy who's never
had to think about his life, and by the completion of
his story in series two, he's fundamentally changed.
He gets stronger, he gets crosser..."
RT, April 2006

TURNCOAT
"Do you really think you can knock out a dinosaur with that thing?"
Just another day at Unit HQ, but Mike (Richard Franklin) was about to
betray the Doctor (Jon Pertwee) in *Invasion of the Dinosaurs* (1974)

CAPTAIN MIKE YATES
Richard Franklin

Dates: 1971–74, 1983
Doctor: Jon Pertwee

The Unit captain had a story arc that was, for the time, imaginative and daring. Standing shoulder to shoulder with the Brigadier, he helped defend the Earth against numerous alien threats. Although his clear soft spot for Jo was undeveloped by the writers, what did emerge was a corruptible streak.

After being brainwashed by a computer called Boss in *The Green Death*, he backed a crackpot ecological scheme in *Invasion of the Dinosaurs*, which involved returning the Earth to a time before humanity turned up to spoil things. He was granted medical leave by Unit, and his rehabilitation led to some useful detective work for the Doctor in *Planet of the Spiders*.

He faded from the series but made a cameo appearance in *The Five Doctors* (1983).

MEMORABLE MOMENT

In the days before major plot points were revealed, this one was a shocker: Mike pulls a gun on Sergeant Benton and the Brig: "And what do you think you're doing, Captain Yates?!" *Invasion of the Dinosaurs* 1974)

OUTWARD BOUND
Above: a rare R' shot of Mike, tied up and gagged a a meditation centre in his leaving story *Planet of the Spider* (1974

NYSSA
Sarah Sutton

Dates: 1981–83
Doctors: Tom Baker, Peter Davison

A gifted scientist, sweet and innocent Nyssa was left orphaned when the Master took over her father's body and subsequently destroyed her home world of Traken. She was originally intended only to appear in one story, but producer John Nathan-Turner immediately saw Nyssa's companion potential and she was hurriedly re-introduced in the fourth Doctor's final story, *Logopolis*.

Nyssa was the most closely attuned companion – intellectually – to the fifth Doctor, although her travels in the Tardis were a time of upheaval, and she was deeply upset by the death of fellow companion Adric. Her unselfish nature came to the fore on the space station Terminus, where she chose to remain, caring for victims of Lazar's disease.

IN THEIR OWN WORDS

"Nyssa is a noble, intelligent Trakenite and an expert in bioelectronics. The costume is lovely, though it's a bit chilly on filming days."
RT, January 1981

"She was a challenge to play and it was great fun trying to get my tongue round all the long, technical words I couldn't pronounce."
RT, 20th Anniversary Special, 1983

CHANGING TIMES
Above: Sarah Sutton welcomed Mark Strickson (Turlough) to the team outside the BBC Rehearsal Rooms in North Acton (1983)
Below: Nyssa in her debut story, *The Keeper of Traken* (1981)

MEMORABLE MOMENT

In a story set in interwar England, Sarah Sutton has fun playing both Nyssa and her lookalike Ann Talbot, dancing the charleston and donning fancy dress. (*Black Orchid*, 1982)

YOUTHFUL TEAM
"Got to be fit to crew the Tardis. A trim timeship and a shipshape team," insisted the newly regenerated fifth Doctor in *Castrovalva*. *RT* captured Janet Fielding, Peter Davison, Matthew Waterhouse and Sarah Sutton on location at Buckhurst Park, East Sussex in September 1981

"It was great fun trying to
get my tongue round all the
long, technical words"
SARAH SUTTON, *RT 1983*

PERI BROWN
Nicola Bryant

Dates: 1984–86
Doctors: Peter Davison, Colin Baker

Perpugilliam Brown, Peri for short, was an American botany student on vacation in Lanzarote who was rescued from drowning by Turlough. He carried her aboard the Tardis to recover, where she had a nasty encounter with the robotic Kamelion.

A bright young woman, Peri had only just started to get to know the fifth Doctor, when she contracted spectrox toxaemia in *The Caves of Androzani*. The Time Lord gave up another of his lives to save her. After a swift regeneration, the sixth Doctor's cantankerous nature and Peri's impulse to whinge made for an uneasy rapport.

They tackled Cybermen, the Master and the Rani, and in *The Two Doctors*, Peri encountered yet another Doctor (Patrick Troughton) and his companion, Jamie (Frazer Hines).

During his second trial by the Time Lords, the Doctor was distressed to learn of Peri's death: the slug-like Kiv had transplanted his mind into her body. The story turned out to be false; in fact she'd married warrior king Yrcanos (Brian Blessed).

Critics complained about the dubious rationale for introducing Peri and her skimpy outfits. But the same thing had been said before about Leela, and has been said of subsequent sidekicks. Nicola Bryant played Peri with an American accent, but was actually born in Surrey.

IN THEIR OWN WORDS

"When I was about 12, I remember coming home one afternoon, switching on *Doctor Who*, and saying to my parents that it was going to be my first job, even though I hadn't finally decided then I wanted to be an actress."
***RT*, 20th Anniversary Special, 1983**

"I suggested I should be dropped off where I was originally found, which was in the sea, drowning."
***RT*, September 1986**

"I lied my way onto the show! I had dual nationality, but I'm not American, although I can do a convincing accent. At least, it convinced the producer and everyone else on the programme."
***RT*, May 1996**

RADIO TIME
In 1985, when BBC1 "rested" the series for 18 months, Colin Baker and Nicola Bryant made *Slipback*, a *Doctor Who* serial for Radio 4

"For about two years after, I could only get parts playing Americans, although I was born in Surrey"

NICOLA BRYANT, *RT NOVEMBER 1988*

MEMORABLE MOMENT
Peri's transformation into a bird-like creature, requiring elaborate make-up. "Just to add to the fun, I was allergic to feathers," said Bryant later. (*Vengeance on Varos*, 1985)

POLLY
Anneke Wills

Dates: 1966–67
Doctors: William Hartnell, Patrick Troughton

Blonde, heavily mascara-ed, curvaceous and posh, Polly was arguably the first *Doctor Who* companion-as-totty, and reflected the Swinging Sixties better than any of her predecessors.

In London 1966, she had a cool job as personal secretary to Professor Brett at the newly opened Post Office Tower. At the hottest nightspot in town, the Inferno, Polly hooked up with cockney sailor Ben, who insisted on calling her "Duchess". They let themselves aboard the Tardis with Dodo's key, and set off on adventures with smugglers, Highlanders, Atlanteans and, of course, the Daleks.

Perhaps more than Ben, Polly instinctively had faith in the Doctor after he first changed his appearance: "It *is* the Doctor. I know it is!" A healthy screamer, she was also resourceful – once defeating the Cybermen with a solvent based on nail-varnish remover.

After being duplicated by the faceless Chameleons at Gatwick Airport, Polly decided to stay in 1966 with Ben. She bid the Doctor a tearful farewell: "You will be safe, won't you?" Many years later, in *The Sarah Jane Adventures* (2010), we learnt that Ben and Polly were still together and running an orphanage in India.

SILVER SURFERS
Main picture: Ben and Polly were the earliest companions to fend off the Cybermen. In 1973, actors Anneke Wills and Michael Craze were reunited with the deadly cyborgs on the Norfolk coast for *RT's 10th Anniversary Special*

"I wanted to be a sort of feminine anti-hero, a weedy, frightened lady who screamed and kicked and shouted 'Doctor!' at the least sign of danger"

ANNEKE WILLS, *RT 1973*

"The series was much more 'me' when Patrick Troughton took over. I always felt it should have been played more for comedy"

ANNEKE WILLS, *RT 1973*

OUT THERE
Above: Polly (Anneke Wills) and Ben (Michael Craze) got all steamed up in *The Moonbase* (1967)

Left: "Oh dear, all this distraction! And I really thought I was going to be alone again." The first Doctor (William Hartnell) adjusted to new arrivals Ben and Polly in *The Smugglers* (1966)

IN THEIR OWN WORDS

"I wanted to play her like myself – scatterbrained, or 'kooky', as the newspapers persisted in calling me. I thought it would be a very good idea to play a total coward. Television was full of brave ladies in those days. I wanted to be a sort of feminine anti-hero, a weedy, frightened lady who screamed and kicked and shouted 'Doctor!' at the least sign of danger. I think Polly got a bit braver towards the end."
RT, 10th Anniversary Special, 1973

"My own children got wound up in it. One day, while I was away rehearsing, they saw an episode in which I was carried off by monsters. They were very worried about whether I was going to come home that night."
RT, 10th Anniversary Special, 1973

"I decided not to play a Diana Rigg macho character, and to be real: very scared, but very brave. So Polly goes up to the Cyberman and says, 'But don't you care?' It was terribly sweet really."
RT, November 1999

MEMORABLE MOMENT

Just after the Battle of Culloden, Polly and her pal Kirsty (Hannah Gordon) use their feminine wiles to blackmail "Algy, dear" – the lily-livered Lieutenant Algernon ffinch (Michael Elwyn) – into helping them track down the Doctor.
(*The Highlanders*, 1966)

"I thought I'd died, but I didn't. Well, I haven't yet. God, it's complicated!"

ALEX KINGSTON, *RT May 2010*

Alex Kingston

Dates: from 2008
Doctors: David Tennant, Matt Smith

A professor, archaeologist, jailbird, *femme fatale* primed with hallucinogenic lipstick... But who is River Song really? When the tenth Doctor first met River on the Library planet, she already knew him intimately ("Hello, sweetie!"). She was even aware of his real name – the mystery at the heart of *Doctor Who* since the series began. Her blue diary had tempting "Spoilers!" on all their unseen adventures. And then she died: electrocuting herself to protect the Doctor (although he managed to save her "data ghost" so that she could live on in a virtual reality).

But that was not the last he'd see of her. When River surfaced again at the crash of the *Byzantium*, the 11th Doctor told Amy, "We keep meeting in the wrong order." She could pilot the Tardis, helped fend off the Weeping Angels and admitted she'd killed "a very good man, the best man I've ever known".

Then, later for the Doctor but earlier for her, River turned up again when Winston Churchill asked her to pass on a warning to the Doctor. He found her in Roman Britain, disguised as Cleopatra, in the events that led up to the Pandorica opening.

After all that, River Song remains an enigma. "Who is she really?" teased showrunner Steven Moffat on *Doctor Who Confidential* in June 2010. "That's what we're gonna find out next year."

SONG OF LOVE
Above: the tenth Doctor (David Tennant) was unnerved by River (Alex Kingston) in *The Silence in the Library* (2008), but the 11th Doctor (Matt Smith) was beginning to get a handle on her "Spoilers!" by *The Time of Angels* (2010), below

SHE'S A MYSTERY
River Song (Alex Kingston) darts in
and out of the Doctor's destiny,
always changing her image. From top:
in army fatigues in *Flesh and Stone*,
full *femme fatale* get-up in *The Time
of Angels* and contemporary casuals
in *The Pandorica Opens*

"It's scary stuff, but quite esoteric in places. Grown-ups will be scared, too! On *ER*, I'd work with a medical consultant, who'd explain what we were saying, so I'd say it with a purpose and a truth. On *Doctor Who*, I've no idea what some of my lines mean. David [Tennant] is brilliant at it, though. He seems to understand every word."
RT, May 2008

"I thought I'd died, but I didn't. Well, I did, but I haven't yet. God, it's complicated! The flirtation between them still indicates they have a much more intimate relationship further down the line – and I sort of hope it is that. I hope they're married. Otherwise, if she is his mother, the flirtation isn't quite appropriate! She could be the Doctor's grandmother, for goodness' sake!"
RT, May 2010

> "I hope they're married. Otherwise, if she is his mother, the flirtation isn't quite appropriate!"
> ALEX KINGSTON, *RT May 2010*

MEMORABLE MOMENT
River knows how to make an exit – *and* an entrance. "You might want to find something to hang on to," she tells her captors on the *Byzantium* before blasting across space to the waiting Tardis and flattening the Doctor. (*The Time of Angels*, 2010)

ROMANA I
Mary Tamm

Dates: 1978–79
Doctor: Tom Baker

Romana, or Romanadvoratrelundar, was a Time Lady assigned by the White Guardian to help the fourth Doctor in his quest for the Key to Time. Classy, refined and "nearly 140" years old, she'd graduated from the Academy with a triple first and considered the Doctor her intellectual inferior.

He was soon able to trump her with his depth of knowledge and first-hand experience, although he was often annoyed by her facility with the Tardis controls. Her regal air stood her in good stead during their travels, until they arrived on Tara where she was mistaken for her identical double, the Princess Strella.

Disenchanted with Romana's lack of character development, Mary Tamm flatly refused to return for a second series, although she claims to have suggested Lalla Ward as her replacement.

"I'm supposed to be bright, sophisticated and cool, but as I've only just qualified from the Academy, I have a lot to learn."
RT, September 1978

Tom Baker: "It's always a worry when a new girl takes over. But all the roles seem to have been successful. I've enjoyed working with Lis [Sladen] and Louise [Jameson] – as now I'm enjoying working with Mary." And on the possibility of hanky panky: "It would be an absolute disaster to have an emphasis like that. The Doctor must be above any emotional involvement. His only task is to stamp out evil and fight for good."
RT, September 1978

"When I took on Romana, the idea was that she would become as important as the Doctor – a partner rather than just a companion. That never materialised because the plots required someone to ask questions all the time."
RT, November 1988

LORD AND LADY
Main picture:
RT photographed
Tom Baker and
Mary Tamm in 1978
ahead of the 16th
season of *Doctor Who*

MEMORABLE MOMENT
Irritated by Romana's haughtiness from the word go, the Doctor is mortified to find she's had the temerity to tamper with his beloved control console. "A hole! What's a hole doing in my Tardis?" "I put it there," she replies airily. (*The Ribos Operation*, 1978)

"The Doctor must be above any emotional involvement"
TOM BAKER, *RT SEPTEMBER 1978*

ROMANA II
Lalla Ward

Dates: 1979–81
Doctor: Tom Baker

Apparently tired of her old body, Romana decided to regenerate and paraded a variety of interim new looks in front of the Doctor, before settling on the likeness of Princess Astra, whom they'd met in *The Armageddon Factor*. It was a neat way of recasting Lalla Ward, who'd proven popular in the previous adventure.

This new Romana was a friendlier, more ebullient incarnation, better matched to the Fourth Doctor, and something of a clothes' horse. She even designed her own slimline sonic screwdriver. They finally parted company in E-Space, as Romana stayed behind to liberate the leonine Tharils with the help of K•9. "You were the noblest Romana of them all," the Doctor called after her.

In real life, Lalla Ward and Tom Baker had a short-lived marriage (1980–82); since 1992 she's been married to evolutionary biologist Richard Dawkins.

"I regard the definitive *Doctor Who* as the one when she was there"

RICHARD DAWKINS, LALLA WARD'S HUSBAND, *RT 2008*

LAZY DAYS
Above: lying back in a Cambridge punt in *Shada*, a six-part serial by Douglas Adams that was never completed due to a strike at the BBC in 1979

TIME AND TIDE
Left: a nautical-looking Lalla Ward filming in Brighton, March 1980. In *The Leisure Hive* at the start of season 18, the Doctor and Romana were evading the Black Guardian. "I shouldn't think even he fancies freezing to death on Brighton beach!" she complained

Costume designer **June Hudson**: "Lalla is very different from Mary [Tamm]. She's young and girlish, whereas Mary was cool, elegant and remote, so I've designed playful, witty clothes for her. I've given her a pink copy, a take-off, of Doctor Who's clothes – even with her own long scarf, but made of silk."
RT, September 1979

Richard Dawkins appeared briefly as himself in *Doctor Who* in 2008. But whose performance was better – his or his wife's? "Well, obviously hers! We were introduced by Douglas Adams; she knew him because he was a scriptwriter on *Doctor Who* during her time. I regard the definitive *Doctor Who* as the one when she was there. I don't have any truck with this modern version."
RT, August 2008

MR AND MRS WHO
Lalla Ward and Tom Baker tied the knot in 1980 at Chelsea Register Office

MEMORABLE MOMENT
On a romantic break in Paris, Romana ponders whether they should descend from the Eiffel Tower by lift or by flying. "Let's not be ostentatious," warns the Doctor. "All right. Let's fly then," says Romana – possibly in earnest. (*City of Death*, 1979)

"When I started on *Doctor Who*, I never thought I'd get the chance to be a Roman soldier. It was a bit like wearing a one-man band. It just made so much noise"

ARTHUR DARVILL, *RT NOVEMBER 2010*

IN THEIR OWN WORDS

Working with Matt Smith: "We did a play together and we know a lot of the same people, so we always said we wanted to work together again. I never thought it would be for quite so long! And it's been brilliant – doing a job like this but also with someone who's a friend."
RT, November 2010

On being newlyweds in the Tardis: "Rory was striving to get Amy down the aisle. That's what his whole life up to that point was geared towards, and now it's like they've got all the wonders of the universe to explore as well. I don't think it's an anticlimax – for him. He feels far more secure in their relationship, but it doesn't stop them carrying on their adventures and exploring even further."
RT, November 2010

"Oh man, what have been the coolest moments? Walking into the Tardis and seeing it all frosted over by the Dream Lord [*Amy's Choice*]. And I think one of my most enjoyable moments was doing the swordfight with Alex Price in Croatia [*The Vampires of Venice*]. That was really good fun. I really enjoyed the day where I had a gun come out of my hand and got to shoot a Dalek in the face [*The Big Bang*]. That was a big private moment for me."
RT, November 2010
See extended interview at
radiotimes.com/arthur-darvill

THE DEATH AND LIFE OF RORY WILLIAMS
Rory's luck ran out during an encounter with the Silurians in the 2010 two-parter *The Hungry Earth/Cold Blood* (below), but he returned, first as a Nestene duplicate in *The Pandorica Opens* (right), then as a human being again in *The Big Bang* when the timeline was restored. Phew!

FILMING AT STONEHENGE
"We were filming at night, so I drove myself there in my car," recalled Arthur Darvill in November 2010. "It was really dark and then I just saw the whole of Stonehenge completely lit up by all the *Doctor Who* crew lights. It was just like this big shaft of light coming up off Stonehenge. It was absolutely amazing. Ever so slightly emotional."

RORY WILLIAMS
Arthur Darvill

Dates: from 2010
Doctor: Matt Smith

Sweet, dependable Rory — Amy's childhood friend forced to play her games about a Raggedy Doctor, only to learn as an adult that the Doctor really existed and could represent a romantic rival.

A nurse at Royal Leadworth Hospital and, by 2010, Amy's fiancé, Rory joined the Tardis more to protect Amy than out of any sense of adventure. Perhaps a bit of a lemon, he's also big-hearted and brave. He admires the Doctor, but is prepared to challenge him. In *The Vampires of Venice*, he told him, "You've no idea how dangerous you make people to themselves when you're around."

Case proven in *Cold Blood*. Rory died defending his friends in the Silurian caves, and was then erased from existence by the crack in time. Miraculously, he was resurrected as a Roman centurion/Nestene duplicate and eventually — via the power of Amy's memories — was restored to his old self in time for their wedding.

As Mr and Mrs Pond (not Williams!) head towards Christmas and adventures with the Doctor in 2011, the chemistry between the Tardis trio is palpable.

Indeed, Arthur Darvill and Matt Smith are old chums. In 2007, they acted together in the West End play *Swimming with Sharks* and were both nominated as outstanding newcomer in the *Evening Standard* Theatre Awards.

MEMORABLE MOMENT

More of a Memorable Two Millennia as Centurion Rory, devoted to Amy, keeps watch over her from Roman times right up to the 21st century while she's encased inside the Pandorica. Now that's love! (*The Big Bang*, 2010)

> "When she meets the Doctor, she gets the chance to show she's better than the life she's been leading"
>
> RUSSELL T DAVIES, *RT MARCH 2005*

ROSE TYLER
Billie Piper

Dates: 2005–2010
Doctors: Christopher Eccleston, David Tennant

PIPER ABOARD
Top: Christopher Eccleston and Billie Piper photographed on the Tardis set, built at Unit Q2 in Newport. A take with different lighting (above) was used for the inside of *RT's* barn door cover in March 2005, which also contained a 16-page pull-out (right)

Gutsy, working-class shop assistant Rose struck such a lasting chord with the public that she has just been voted the Doctor's greatest companion in *RT's* online poll. Her popularity is due not only to Billie Piper's winning performance, but also to Russell T Davies. The way he focused on Rose, when the series returned in 2005, enabled the audience to form an instant rapport with her.

Offered the chance to escape her dead-end job and her drab life on a south London council estate, Rose grabbed it with glee. The streetwise teen had an insatiable appetite to see the universe with the ninth Doctor – and a curiosity that led her into serious trouble, especially when she returned to 1987 and tried to prevent her father Pete's death.

Nothing seemed to faze her: trips to the end of the world and New Earth, or to meet Charles Dickens and Queen Victoria. She formed a strong bond with the Doctor – nursing him through his regeneration into the tenth Doctor – but they were separated when she ensured that all Daleks and Cybermen invading the Earth were sucked into a Void.

In doing so, she was transported to a parallel universe, where she lived with her mum Jackie, on/off boyfriend Mickey and an alternate version of her father. After her various attempts to send a message to the Doctor from her new home, they were reunited in defeating the New Dalek Empire. A half-human duplicate Doctor became her companion on parallel Earth.

The last time we saw Rose was when an ailing tenth Doctor returned to her estate on New Year's Day, 2005 – a point before they'd first met. "I bet you're going to have a really great year," he told her.

ONE OF A KIND
Rose displayed her unique
qualities as a companion
in *Dalek* (2005) by showing
compassion for the last
remaining example of
the Doctor's iconic foe.
Unfortunately, her
"touching" sympathy
brought the metal monster
back to life! The episode
was filmed between October
and November 2004 at
the show's Newport studios,
as well as Cardiff's
National Museum and
Millennium Stadium

UNDERCOVER STORY
From a rough sketch drawn by *RT*, the *Doctor Who* production team made a scaled-down model of the set. It depicted the fictional Powell Estate in London where Rose lived. The actors were shot on the full-scale set in Cardiff and voilà! – a triple gatefold cover setting out the store of season two in 2006

And they're not alone ... open here to see who's joining them ▶   **Sarah Jane, K-9** (episode three)   **Sister of Plenitude** (episode one)   **Clockwork robots** (episode four)   **Cyberman** (episode five)

BRIDGE STREET SE15
LONDON BOROUGH OF SOUTHWARK

NO BALL GAMES
POWER ESTATE

IN THEIR OWN WORDS

"She's on a par with the Doctor. They teach each other. She's quite closed off from the world, but could, potentially, be someone brilliant. He shows her how to do that. And equally, she shows him how to be sympathetic, how to have morals and express his emotions. It's an interesting dynamic."
RT, March 2005

Russell T Davies: "She's got a dead-end job and a boring boyfriend; she lives with her mum on a rundown estate – but when she meets the Doctor, she gets the chance to show she's better than the life she's been leading."
RT, March 2005

Christopher Eccleston: "He loves her, simple as that. And she loves him. They both deny it, but her mother can see it. They're very similar, Rose and the Doctor. Both carry a sense of loneliness. He allows her freedom – he's always encouraging her to experience things – but he expects a great deal of her, too."
RT, March 2005

IT MUST BE LOVE?
Top: "I think you need a Doctor," said ninth Doctor
Christopher Eccleston, orally drawing lethal time vortex
energy from Rose in *The Parting of the Ways* (2005).
Above: possessed by Cassandra, Rose smooched tenth
Doctor David Tennant in *New Earth* (2006)

Russell T Davies: "Rose really becomes a seasoned space traveller in this series [two]. I don't want to give too much away, but if you watch the Doctor and Rose closely, there's an overconfidence that could well be their downfall."
RT, April 2006

"Do we have nicknames for each other? Yeah... this is going to start so much havoc. I recently named him David Ten-inch. I have no basis or grounds for calling him that. I just find it funny."
RT, April 2006

On leaving: "The longer I stayed, the more scared I'd be about leaving because it's so comfortable and nice. I'm utterly grateful for the whole experience, but you have to take care of yourself and do what you feel is right."
RT, July 2006

Russell T Davies: "It's certainly some sort of love, but I think sometimes this gets massively overstated. If you look at all the lovey-dovey dialogue between them, over two years and 27 episodes, it amounted to three slight hints and no proper kiss."
RT, June 2008

"She shows the Doctor how to have morals and express his emotions"

BILLIE PIPER, *RT MARCH 2005*

ROSE BLOSSOMS
Above left: on *New Earth* (2006) in the year five billion and twenty-three Rose and Chip, a forced-grown clone (Sean Gallagher), acted as hosts for "bitchy trampoline" Lady Cassandra

Left: Rose and her on/off boyfriend Mickey Smith (Noel Clarke) enjoyed the festive period before it all began to go pear-shaped in *The Christmas Invasion* (2005)

MEMORABLE MOMENT

Proof, if any were needed, that the rebooted series wasn't afraid to go for the emotional jugular. The Doctor sends his farewells to Rose through the closing gap between the real and parallel worlds. Through floods of tears, Rose tells him, "I love you," but he doesn't get the chance to reply... (*Doomsday*, 2006)

CAPTURED IN TIME (IN 2006)

Top: in *The Satan Pit*, Rose used a boltgun to eject a Beast-possessed human from her escape rocket

Above: filming *Doomsday's* unforgettable departure scene in Bad Wolf Bay – actually Dunraven Bay, Southerndown, near Bridgend, in January. Brrrr!

Left: Rose discovered that time travel with the Doctor (David Tennant) is the new rock 'n' roll in *The Idiot's Lantern*

POLL POSITION
Our cover shot in June 2008 was almost prophetic: Rose was voted
the number one companion in *RT's* online poll of more than 3,000 readers.
Donna (Catherine Tate) came third, while Martha (Freema Agyeman) was 11th.
The actors were shot separately in Cardiff and their images assembled later

THE ULTIMATE DIGITAL TV AND RADIO GUIDE
WIMBLEDON
STARTS HERE!

RadioTimes
www.radiotimes.com

WIN
a ride with the Stig!
Top Gear: p26

21–27 JUNE 2008 £1.05

RT EXCLUSIVE
**SHE'S
BACK!**
As Rose returns, Russell T Davies gives
the lowdown on the Doctor's women
Doctor Who, Saturday BBC1

REGAL INTRODUCTION
Eight months before playing Sara, Jean
Marsh was Princess Joanna (right) in
The Crusade alongside Maureen O'Brien
(Vicki) and William Hartnell's Doctor

SARA KINGDOM
Jean Marsh

Dates: 1965–66 **Doctor:** William Hartnell

Space Security Service agent Sara Kingdom appeared in nine episodes of the
12-part epic *The Daleks' Master Plan*. Described by archvillain Mavic Chen as
"ruthless, hard, efficient", she was tasked with hunting down and killing the
Doctor and his party. She gunned down her own brother, the agent Bret Vyon
(Nicholas Courtney), but soon changed sides to join the Tardis crew.

Her travels took her to swampy Mira, volcanic Tigus, Ancient Egypt and even
silent-era Hollywood, where she complained, "A strange man kept telling me
to take my clothes off!" Brave Sara met her end during a showdown with the
Daleks on the planet Kembel (see opposite).

Jean Marsh had previously appeared in *Doctor Who* as Princess Joanna
in *The Crusade* (1965) and returned as Morgaine in the seventh Doctor story
Battlefield (1989). She was once married to third Doctor Jon Pertwee, and
is better known for co-creating and starring in *Upstairs, Downstairs*.

RUTHLESS
Sara Kingdom (Jean Marsh)
was like a space-age
Avengers woman

> ## "I wore a tin box slung round my shoulders... It usually contained my dressing room key, some chewing gum and a half-eaten sandwich"
>
> JEAN MARSH, *RT 1983*

IN THEIR OWN WORDS

"I loved the way they killed me off, exposing me to the dreaded time destructor, which meant I grew rapidly older, and rotted away within a matter of seconds! I loved doing it – and a terrible amount of giggling went on. My costume was a sort of brown tweed space suit, and I wore a tin box slung round my shoulders, which was meant to contain my space tool kit. It usually contained my dressing room key, some chewing gum and a half-eaten sandwich."
RT, 20th Anniversary Special, 1983

ARTHURIAN ROLE
Jean Marsh as Morgaine in 1989

123

INTRODUCING SARAH JANE SMITH
Right: pursued by a Sontaran at Peckforton Castle, Cheshire. This recently rediscovered image from *RT's 10th Anniversary Special* shoot has never been printed full-frame before. Health and safety might now have something to say about the sheer drop!

Below: a cold-looking Elisabeth Sladen at her first press call at BBC TV Centre, 1973

SARAH JANE SMITH
Elisabeth Sladen
Dates: 1973–76, 1981, 1983, from 2006
Doctors: Jon Pertwee, Tom Baker, David Tennant, Matt Smith

Until November 2010, Sarah Jane Smith was *the* greatest companion, as decided by *RT's* 2003 online poll. But she was dethroned by our updated survey, which nudged her into a creditable second place.

In any case, it says much for her immense popularity with viewers that Sladen was invited to reprise her role in *Doctor Who* after a 30-year hiatus (bar two short engagements in the 1980s) – and, of course, to star in her own spin-off series, *The Sarah Jane Adventures*. In the latter she joined forces for one story with her predecessor as *Doctor Who* companion, Jo Grant (Katy Manning).

An inquisitive and determined journalist, Sarah had a knack for finding trouble. The actress ran into serious trouble, too, when filming in the underground lakes of Wookey Hole for 1975's accident-prone story *Revenge of the Cybermen*. She was forced to jump from an out-of-control boat, but struggled in the strong undercurrents, so stuntman Terry Walsh had to dive in to rescue her.

Sarah helped the third Doctor ease into his fourth incarnation, and had terrifying encounters with giant spiders, robotic mummies, carnivorous plants and human-sized insects. Her robust sense of humour saw her through them all. Once, after she was freed from the control of a crystalline alien named Eldrad, she teased the Doctor by continuing to say, "Eldrad must live." It was unquestionably a special relationship, best summed up by the Doctor when he declared, "She's my best friend."

> "I don't mind monsters like the Daleks, but it's the little moving things that frighten me. I hate creepies"
>
> ELISABETH SLADEN, *RT 1973*

SMITH REPORT
Top: arachnophobes look away! Sarah visited Metebelis 3 and encountered the Queen of the Eight Legs – *Planet of the Spiders* (1974)

Left: "What are you making?" In Sarah's second story, *Invasion of the Dinosaurs* (1974), the third Doctor (Jon Pertwee) prepared a device to knock out a brontosaurus

Right: a rare *RT* shot from a *Planet of the Spiders* camera rehearsal, showing Jon Pertwee and Elisabeth Sladen before they'd changed into their characters' costumes

IN THEIR OWN WORDS

"I'm easily spooked. I don't mind monsters like the Daleks, but it's the little moving things that frighten me. I hate creepies. But then I think Sarah Jane Smith, the young journalist I play, does need a bit of protection. She'll always have a bash at things, believing she's right, but somebody normally ends up telling her she's totally wrong – usually the Doctor."
RT, 10th Anniversary Special, 1973

"One of the things I'll have to watch is my accent – or what's left of it. Until I went to drama school I had a pronounced Liverpool accent, though not as thick as Cilla Black's. I still have a sing-song accent and it comes though in times of stress."
RT, 10th Anniversary Special, 1973

"I may be biased but I think my series was the best. There is a very fine line between fantasy and fear, and they got it right in my time. I have nothing but happy memories of the series – but I certainly wasn't the Doctor's equal."
RT, September 1978

On Pertwee and Baker: "They're both very good actors and very strong personalities in their own ways, which gave me something different to bounce off. It helps when you have to say, 'Yes, Doctor', 'No, Doctor' a lot of the time."
RT, 20th Anniversary Special, 1983

Producer, **John Nathan-Turner:** "The big change in the Doctor's companions came in 1973. Sarah was much more independently minded. She was fiercely loyal to the Doctor but always spoke her mind. After Sarah, it would have been impossible to go back to the old kind of companions."
RT, November 1988

On being voted best companion in *RT's* 2003 poll: "I'm thrilled Sarah Jane Smith is still so popular. I had a ball working on *Doctor Who*. It was only after I left that I realised what an incredible impact it had."
RT, 40th Anniversary Special, 2003

**SARAH JANE
IN JEOPARDY**
Right: Sarah was
menaced by Ice Warrior
commander Azaxyr
(Alan Bennion) in
*The Monster of
Peladon* (1974)

Below: it was a landmark
moment when Sarah
and Harry (Ian Marter)
witnessed the Doctor
(Tom Baker) agonising
over ridding the universe
for ever of his mortal
enemy in *Genesis of
the Daleks* (1975)

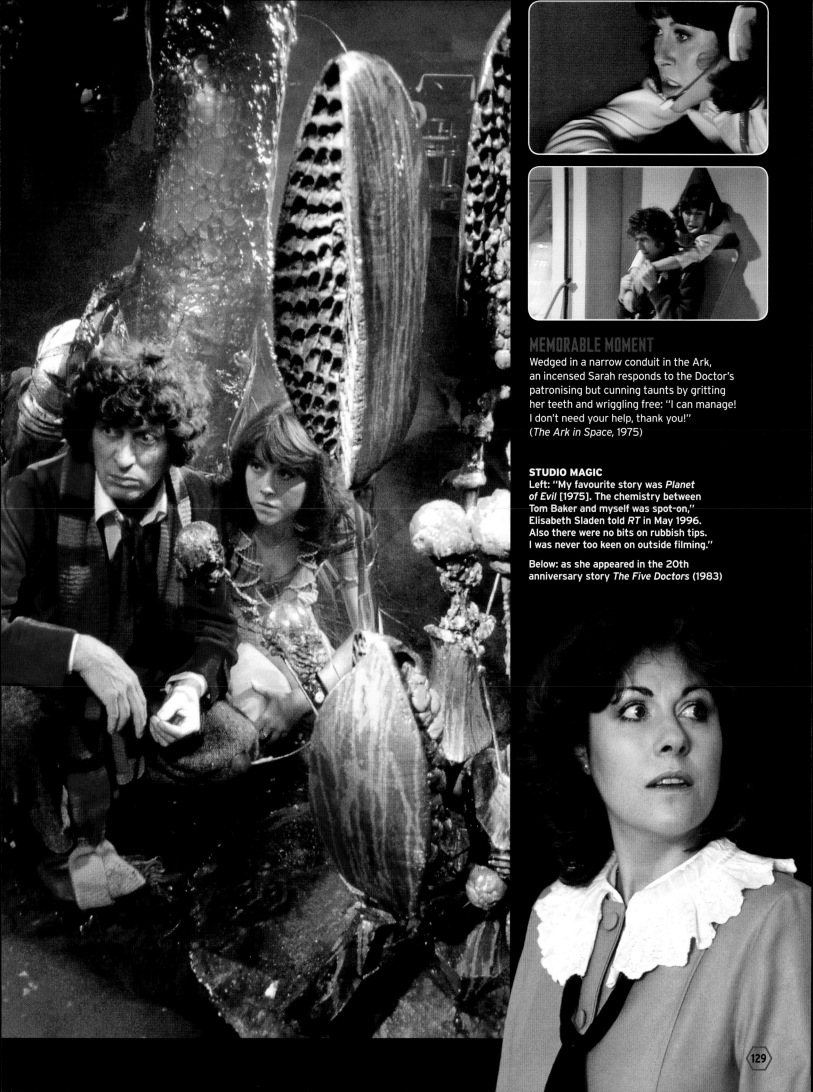

MEMORABLE MOMENT

Wedged in a narrow conduit in the Ark, an incensed Sarah responds to the Doctor's patronising but cunning taunts by gritting her teeth and wriggling free: "I can manage! I don't need your help, thank you!" (*The Ark in Space*, 1975)

STUDIO MAGIC
Left: "My favourite story was *Planet of Evil* [1975]. The chemistry between Tom Baker and myself was spot-on," Elisabeth Sladen told *RT* in May 1996. Also there were no bits on rubbish tips. I was never too keen on outside filming."

Below: as she appeared in the 20th anniversary story *The Five Doctors* (1983)

Russell T Davies: "Elisabeth Sladen as Sarah Jane was loved not just by fans, but by a whole generation. Plus – and I'm not kidding – she looks exactly the same. You want that visceral shock of people saying, 'Oh my God, it's her!'"
RT, April 2006

"I walked away from this character, but she never walked away from me. My agent phoned up and said that Russell T Davies and Phil Collinson wanted to take me out for a meal to talk about *Doctor Who*. We got on so well, it became a very rowdy table, probably too much to drink, and I agreed to do it. They had such a love of the programme and I just thought, 'What a challenge!'"
RT, April 2006

Matt Smith: "I'm constantly aware of *Doctor Who's* rich history. There's a line in my Sarah Jane episodes that refers to a ventilation shaft – when Lis was Tom Baker's assistant her character got stuck in a lift shaft [see page 129]. So my line is: 'Ventilation shaft... that takes me back – or maybe it's forward.' So I'm aware of the heritage and aware too that I am just another stage in this very brilliant and wonderful show."
RT, October 2010

A PROPER HUG AT LAST
Above and left: shooting the episode *School Reunion* (2006): "I waited for you and you didn't come back," she told the tenth Doctor (David Tennant). "Everyone died, Sarah," he confided. In the 21st century, it seems only the Doctor can still get away with calling her "Sarah" and not "Sarah Jane"

FRIENDS REUNITED
Above and right: the Doctor had something to say when his "best friend" decided to get married in her spin-off series *The Sarah Jane Adventures*. *RT* was on the Tardis set in 2009 to capture them – plus K•9!

"Elisabeth Sladen as Sarah Jane was loved not just by fans, but by a whole generation"

RUSSELL T DAVIES, *RT APRIL 2006*

OLD FRIENDS
RT caught the moment when Jo Jones (Katy Manning) and Sarah Jane Smith (Elisabeth Sladen) hooked up with 11th Doctor Matt Smith in *The Sarah Jane Adventures* (2010)

FAMILY UNIT
Sgt Benton, Mike Yates, the Doctor, the Brigadier and Sarah Jane Smith receiving updates on the *Invasion of the Dinosaurs* (1974)

SERGEANT BENTON

John Levene

Dates: 1968–75
Doctors: Patrick Troughton, Jon Pertwee, Tom Baker

Rising through the ranks from Corporal, to Sergeant and eventually RSM, Benton (we'd never discover his first name on screen) was a capable soldier, somewhat shy but not beyond dishing out mild sarcasm to his superiors, the Brigadier and Captain Yates.

He was one of the few people to get away with calling the Doctor "Doc" and once almost outsmarted the Master. During the dinosaur invasion of London, he even grappled with the rogue General Finch: "Not many sergeants get the chance to punch a general on the nose!" Benton faded from the series in 1975 and the Brigadier later revealed that he'd become a car salesman.

John Levene had started 1960s *Doctor Who* as a stuntman/extra playing a Cyberman and a Yeti, until director Douglas Camfield cast him as a corporal and gradually built up Levene's part, and his confidence, as a Unit regular.

MEMORABLE MOMENT

A temporal experiment accidentally transforms Benton into a baby. Later, time reverts and – much to the amusement of his friends – the mortified sergeant rises naked from a nappy. "Would somebody please mind telling me exactly what's happening around here?" A saucy end to the ninth season.
(*The Time Monster*, 1972)

STEVEN TAYLOR
Peter Purves

Dates: 1965–66
Doctor: William Hartnell

Many forget that prior to his decade-long stint as an iconic *Blue Peter* presenter, Peter Purves spent a year lending solid support as a hero in *Doctor Who*.

Space pilot Steven had been marooned on Mechanus for two years before he found his way aboard the Tardis. An opinionated chap, he often bickered with Vicki, the Doctor and later Dodo, but proved himself brave and resourceful.

Posing as a Greek soldier (right), he was almost mortally wounded during the siege of Troy. Then in *The Massacre of St Bartholomew's Eve*, set in Paris 1572, Steven became a man lost in time, and had to carry virtually an entire story alone after the Doctor vanished. Later, appalled by the Doctor's attitude to the carnage left behind in France, he considered leaving the Tardis. "If your researches have so little regard for human life then I want no part of it."

They settled their differences and Steven eventually departed four months later to lead an alien civilisation (see overleaf).

TAYLOR MADE
Steven (Peter Purves) wore a riot of outfits: as a Greek warrior in this rare shot (above) from *The Myth Makers* (1965) and, below, clowning around in stripes in *The Celestial Toymaker* (1966)

WHEN IN PARIS
Opposite: an *RT* shot of William Hartnell and Peter Purves in a Parisian tavern set for *The Massacre of St Bartholomew's Eve*. Recorded in January 1966 at Riverside Studio 1 in Hammersmith

to the massacre of the Huguenots in France"

Peter Purves, *RT 1973*

066 AND ALL THAT
Vicki (Maureen O'Brien) and Steven (Peter Purves) helped the Doctor (William Hartnell) keep British history on course in *The Time Meddler* (1965)

"I've always been one for action,
which is why I love *Blue Peter* now"

PETER PURVES, *RT 1973*

MEMORABLE MOMENT
An alien race divided into Elders and Savages needs a unifying leader. Steven rises to the

IN THEIR OWN WORDS

"Steven was argumentative and capable of making decisions for himself, if not always the right ones. Quite a together, headstrong young man. I'm sorry to say that he soon became a very watered-down, characterless person, which seemed a great shame. Looking back, I don't think I was very good. When there are monsters around, there's always a tendency to overact, and I did."
RT, 10th Anniversary Special, 1973

"The episode I remember best was *The Celestial Toyroom*, in which Michael Gough played the evil Toymaker. He had contrived a number of games, which the Doctor had to solve or we'd all die. One was the Trilogic Game... that supposedly had magic qualities."
   Purves took the prop home. "Soon afterwards I left *Doctor Who*. I was out of work for more than a year. I'm not a superstitious person, but one day, in desperation, I picked up the Trilogic Game and threw it in the dustbin. I got a job the following week in *Z Cars*, and *Blue Peter* came soon after."
RT, 10th Anniversary Special, 1973

RT. 2980.10.

SUSAN FOREMAN
Carole Ann Ford

Dates: 1963–64, 1983
Doctors: William Hartnell, Richard Hurndall

Nobody was ever closer to the Doctor than his own granddaughter, Susan. Fellow exiles, they were, as he explained in the very first episode of *Doctor Who*, "wanderers in the fourth dimension... cut off from our own planet without friends or protection". And no one would be more at home inside "the Ship" – "I made up the name Tardis from the initials: Time and Relative Dimension in Space," Susan claimed.

When we first saw her, Susan was a pupil at Coal Hill School, trying to live like a normal teenager in London 1963. "I love England in the 20th century. The last five months have been the happiest of my life." Giving her age as 15, she'd borrowed the surname Foreman from a name on the gates of a gloomy junkyard where the Tardis had landed.

Far brainier than the average teenager, Susan occasionally used telepathic powers but was ostensibly childish and prone to shrieking. She matured quickly, however, during *The Dalek Invasion of Earth*, and fell in love with a freedom fighter. Struggling with his emotions, the Doctor double-locked the Tardis doors to prevent Susan entering. He said, "I want you to belong somewhere, to have roots of your own." Thus she was the first companion to leave the series.

A middle-aged Susan was briefly reunited with her grandfather in *The Five Doctors* (1983), with Richard Hurndall replacing the late William Hartnell. They came aboard the Tardis – then occupied by fifth Doctor Peter Davison.

DON'T TIE ME DOWN
Above: a rare, early *RT* shot taken on the set of *The Aztecs* (1964). Against her wishes, Susan (Carole Ann Ford) was chosen to be the bride of a sacrificial victim. "Let him die if he wants to die, but don't ask me to marry him. It's barbaric. I won't do it. I won't!"

FIRST MYSTERY
Printed in *Radio Times* the week before the brand-new series began with *An Unearthly Child* in November 1963, this image of Barbara, Susan and Ian was certainly the first-ever *Doctor Who* photo to appear in the magazine, and probably the first to be published anywhere

58

NEXT WEEK

Dr. Who
SATURDAY's serial begins when two teachers (Jacqueline Hill and William Russell) probe the mystery surrounding one of their pupils (Carol Ann Ford)—and meet the strange Dr. Who

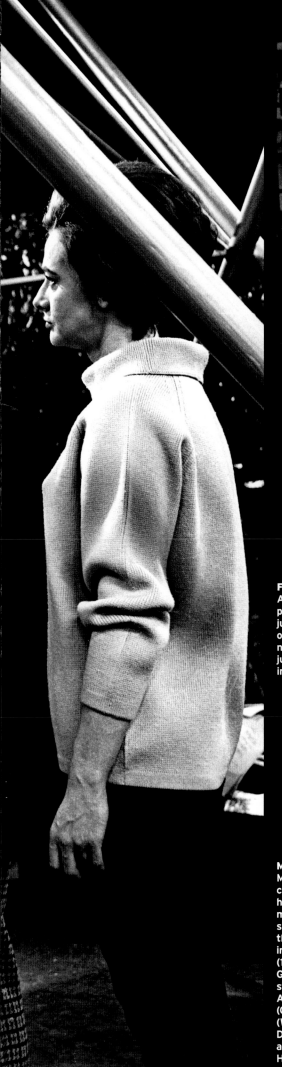

FROM ANOTHER WORLD
Above: Carole Ann Ford posed with a collection of junk to promote the start of *Doctor Who*. This was not the Totters Lane junkyard set that appeared in *An Unearthly Child*

MISSION ON MARINUS
Main picture: "Your coming's brought new hope. Oh yes, yes! You must find the keys for me," said Arbitan, the keeper of the Conscience Machine in *The Keys of Marinus* (1964). He was played by George Coulouris who had starred in *Citizen Kane*. Arbitan sent Susan (Carole Ann Ford), Ian (William Russell), the Doctor (William Hartnell) and Barbara (Jacqueline Hill) on a hazardous six-week quest

IN THEIR OWN WORDS

"Susan was a wonderfully strange character. She was supposed to have an extraordinary intelligence and telepathic communication with the Doctor, her grandfather. I had to have my long hair cropped for the part. Vidal Sassoon cut it to half an inch all over and made it the basis of his cropped-off look that year."
RT, December 1972

"That first story was about the Stone Age and I nearly got eaten alive – but not by monsters. The tropical plants brought into the studio for the set were full of insects. So were the animal skins we had to wear. I had to be fumigated after filming."
RT, 10th Anniversary Special, 1973

"I got the part because I could scream well. I enjoyed the series but had to leave because they wouldn't let me grow up. I was getting older and older but had to stay 15." On modern companions: "Those lovely, sexy, independent parts weren't dreamed of in those days. I had to be childlike and terrified."
RT, September 1978

"I was 21 playing a 15-year-old. When they asked me what qualities were needed for the role, I said you had to be able to scream and run at the same time."
RT, November 1988

William Russell (Ian): "Carole was ideal. She does have a remarkable otherworldly resemblance. She really looked 'not quite one of us'. She felt disappointed because she was just shouting 'Help!' and 'I'm stuck!' She'd thought there was going to be more to the role."
RT, November 2010

FORD FOCUS
An unwieldy camera at Lime Grove Studios recorded the cliffhanger to episode five of *Marco Polo*, when Susan was seized by the merciless Mongol warlord Tegana (Derren Nesbitt)

FUR REAL
Carole Ann Ford had an attack of the Raquel Welches in 1973, when *RT* took her to a prehistoric setting – actually the Crystal Palace Dinosaur Park in south London. This is a rare, alternative shot from the one used in the *10th Anniversary Special*

MEMORABLE MOMENT
The focus of the very first episode, Susan insists to her dumbfounded teachers, Ian and Barbara, "I was born in another time, another world." (*An Unearthly Child*, 1963)

"The tropical plants were full of insects. So were the animal skins we had to wear. I had to be fumigated after filming"

CAROLE ANN FORD, *RT 1973*

WHIZ FROM OZ
Tegan (Janet Fielding) had several new looks throughout her time on *Doctor Who*.

Above: in a taut camisole in *Mawdryn Undead* (1983)

Left: glammed up for *Enlightenment* (1983)

Below: in 80s fashions for *Frontios* (1984)

> ## "Tegan is a mouth on legs! Quite dreadful really"
>
> JANET FIELDING, *RT 1983*

Janet Fielding

Dates: 1981–84
Doctors: Tom Baker, Peter Davison

Chippy, argumentative Tegan was an Australian air stewardess who joined the Doctor in 1981 when she mistook the Tardis for an actual police box. Outwardly headstrong, Tegan was vacillating and insecure. During her travels, she piloted the Tardis, was possessed by serpentine Mara, lost her job, met the Brigadier and witnessed a medieval joust. She met her match in the first Doctor (Richard Hurndall) in *The Five Doctors*. The death toll incurred by the Daleks in 1980s London finally persuaded her to end her travels in the Tardis.

Janet Fielding left acting and became a theatrical agent; she represented Paul McGann in 1996 when he became the eighth Doctor.

In *The Sarah Jane Adventures* (2010), Sarah mentioned that Tegan, whom she had met briefly in *The Five Doctors*, was back in Australia campaigning for Aboriginal rights.

IN THEIR OWN WORDS

"It lets the imagination rip. Earthbound people are anchored to reality. I like being airborne. All theatre should liberate."
RT, February 1981

"Tegan is a mouth on legs! Quite dreadful really."
On her accent: "A lot of Australians don't like it at all. They think it sounds ugly and ask why I don't speak 'nicely' like I normally do. In fact I've toned the accent right down."
RT, 20th Anniversary Special, 1983

"Tegan was bolshy and aggressive and a lot of people could identify with that. The Doctor is, after all, a very irritating person."
RT, May 1996

MEMORABLE MOMENT

The Doctor returns Tegan to Heathrow as promised, but in 1666, prompting the outburst: "That's great. Perhaps I can go out, file a claim on the land. When they get around to inventing the aircraft I'll make a fortune!" (*The Visitation*, 1982)

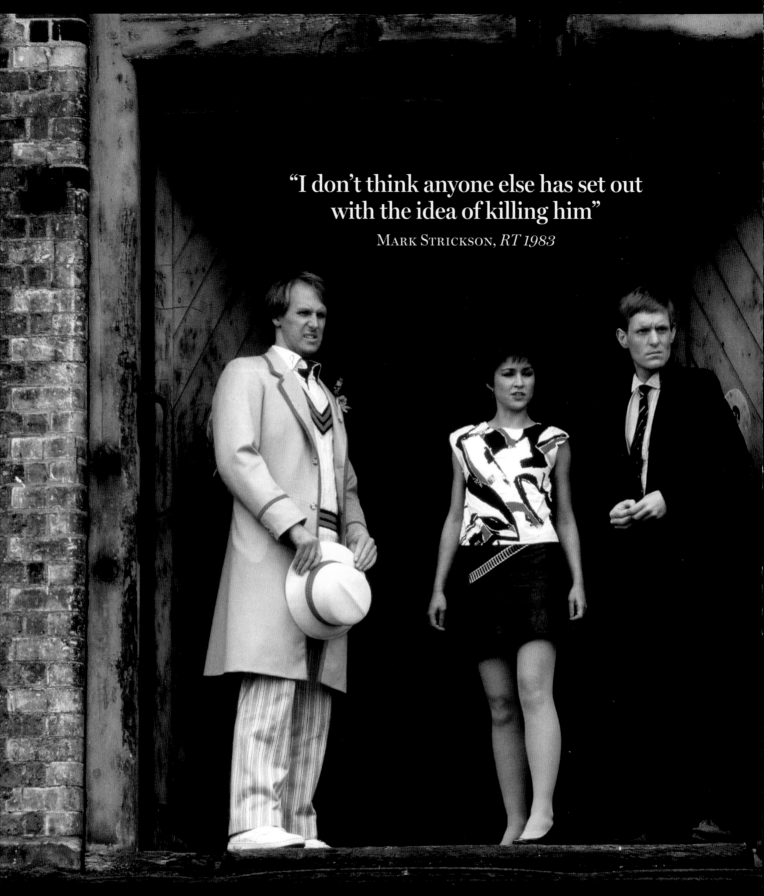

"I don't think anyone else has set out with the idea of killing him"

MARK STRICKSON, *RT 1983*

MEMORABLE MOMENT

Turlough's story arc carries him a long way from the point where he wanted to kill the Doctor. Before finally leaving his mentor, he says, "I don't want to go, Doctor. I've learnt a lot from you." (*Planet of Fire*, 1984)

TURLOUGH
Mark Strickson
Dates: 1983–84
Doctor: Peter Davison

A shifty alien who had been exiled to Earth, Turlough went into hiding in an English public school. Tasked by the Black Guardian with killing the Doctor, Turlough became part of the Tardis crew. He may have been deceitful and secretive, but his heart was never in his various murder attempts. The Doctor's acceptance of Turlough slowly changed the reluctant assassin.

After distancing himself from his evil overlord, he became more selfless and even saved Peri from drowning. In the same adventure, he decided to return to his own planet, Trion, and we learnt that his full name was Vislor Turlough.

IN THEIR OWN WORDS

"He wasn't as predictable as many of the Doctor's other companions have been – I don't think anyone else has set out with the idea of killing him for a start."
RT, 20th Anniversary Special, 1983

BAD BOY
Above: Turlough (Mark Strickson) in his 1983 debut story *Mawdryn Undead* with the Brigadier (Nicholas Courtney) and the Doctor (Peter Davison)

Left: Davison, Janet Fielding and Strickson on location for *Resurrection of the Daleks* (1984). This gloomy Thameside warehouse was soon to become part of the swanky designer-loft development at Butler's Wharf

FRIEND AND FOE
The Doctor and Vicki always hit if off (*The Crusade*, 1965, above), but she couldn't trust duplicitous Koquillion (*The Rescue*, 1965, below)

VICKI
Maureen O'Brien

Dates: 1965 **Doctor:** William Hartnell

The Doctor rescued teenage Vicki from the planet Dido in 2493, where she'd been orphaned after a spaceship crash. She instantly took to the time traveller, telling Ian and Barbara, "As soon as he walked in, I felt that you could trust him. But why does he wear those funny clothes? And that long white hair?"

Replacing the recently departed Susan in the Doctor's affections, Vicki was at his side for encounters with Daleks, Zarbi, Richard the Lionheart, Emperor Nero and the Meddling Monk. She was a plucky youngster but could often be a drip, too.

Maureen O'Brien, now a crime novelist, sometimes derided her feeble scripts and once described Vicki as "an amoeba".

IN THEIR OWN WORDS

William Russell (Ian): "Maureen was marvellous. She didn't compete with Carole [Susan] as an otherworldly character, but was recognisable as a bright young teenager of that period. She's a very intelligent young actress. Well, she's not so young any more. None of us are. She's become a novelist. In fact I went to one of her book launches with Verity [Lambert, *Who's* first producer] a few years back."

CLASSICAL ROLES
In this rare, recently discovered
shot from *The Myth Makers* (1965),
Vicki was hailed as Cressida by King
Priam (Max Adrian) while a sceptical
Cassandra (Frances White) looked on

MEMORABLE MOMENT
Vicki gets arguably the classiest exit from the serie
of any companion. At the siege of Troy, she falls fo
Troilus and – with her name changed to Cressida –
enters mythology (*The Myth Makers*, 1965)

VICTORIA WATERFIELD
Deborah Watling

Dates: 1967–68
Doctor: Patrick Troughton

The Doctor and Jamie took Victoria under their wing after her father's death on the Dalek planet Skaro. A winsome 19th-century maiden, she readily swapped 1860s crinolines for 1960s miniskirts once aboard the Tardis. Occasionally stroppy and intrepid, but mostly quailing, she was eventually overwhelmed by a run of encounters with Daleks, Cybermen, Ice Warriors and Yeti.

Fittingly, in her final adventure, the Doctor used Victoria's amplified screams to overcome an insidious seaweed monster. Jamie was heartbroken when she decided to remain on Earth in the present day with a married couple working at a gas refinery.

HAVING FUN YETI?
Deborah Watling with co-stars Frazer Hines and Patrick Troughton on location in Snowdonia, September 1967, for *The Abominable Snowmen*

"I screamed myself hoarse at every monster that came in sight"

DEBORAH WATLING *RT 1973*

IN THEIR OWN WORDS

"Poor Victoria did have a terrible time one way and another. She was always being scared out of her wits, but I enjoyed it enormously."
RT, April 1969

"I screamed myself hoarse at every monster that came in sight. Victoria became sort of the Doctor's adopted daughter after her father was killed by the Daleks. Patrick, Frazer and I certainly had some fun."
RT, 10th Anniversary Special, 1973

"Patrick and Frazer christened me 'Leatherlungs' because I did so much screaming in the series, though I was more in danger from their practical jokes than I was from the monsters. I had a trunk full of metal dropped behind me when I was meant to be in a trance. I was dropped into a great heap of foam on a freezing winter day on Margate beach... You name it, they did it. But I loved them dearly. It was a smashing two years."
RT, 20th Anniversary Special, 1983

On Yeti: "They were absolutely huge. They used to come up and cuddle me because it was so cold. One of them took me out for a meal."
RT, 40th Anniversary Special, 2003

CLASSIC FOES
Victoria (Deborah Watling) met them all. Opposite page: *The Ice Warriors* and *The Evil of the Daleks* (1967)

Main picture: Frazer Hines and Watling were pursued by a Yeti for this unused shot from *RT's 10th Anniversary Special* photoshoot

MEMORABLE MOMENT

Rose Tyler wasn't the first companion to have a tearful beach farewell. At her wits' end after numerous spine-chilling adventures, Victoria chokes back the tears as she waves goodbye to the Doctor and Jamie. (*Fury from the Deep*, 1968)

"Bernard Bresslaw who played Varga, the chief Ice Warrior, had to carry me off to his ice cave, but since he couldn't see out of his helmet, I had to hiss instructions. Once he misheard me, and walked straight through the wall!"

DEBORAH WATLING, *RT 1983*

WILFRED MOTT
Bernard Cribbins

Dates: 2007–2010
Doctor: David Tennant

A children's favourite across five decades (*The Railway Children, Jackanory, The Wombles*...), Bernard Cribbins had first travelled in the Tardis as policeman Tom Campbell, opposite Peter Cushing's Doctor in the 1966 Dalek movie.

Forty-one years later, he returned in a cameo role as chirpy London news vendor Wilf, who met the tenth Doctor and Astrid during the Christmas special, *Voyage of the Damned*.

After the death of Howard Attfield, the actor who had played Donna Noble's father, Wilf was reintroduced to the series as her grandad. An old soldier, unashamed to show emotion, he was often to be found on his allotment gazing at the stars through his telescope, and danced with joy to spot Donna flying across the night sky in the Tardis.

"I thought it'd be cleaner," he sniffed, checking out the Tardis interior for himself, when at last he got a chance to journey into space. In effect Wilf became the Time Lord's most elderly human companion.

During his final hours, the Doctor realised his fate was inextricably linked to Donna's grandad. Wilf knocked four times, thus fulfilling the prophecy that led to the tenth Doctor's demise.

MEMORABLE MOMENT

A Dalek tries to round up Wilf and his daughter Sylvia (Jacqueline King), but the old soldier refuses to be taken. "Will I 'eck!" He bravely raises a paint gun in a bid to blind the Dalek. The plan doesn't quite succeed... (*The Stolen Earth*, 2008)

"When I told some of the younger ones on the *Doctor Who* team that I was in *Daleks – Invasion Earth 2150 AD* and that it was made 42 years ago, some of them almost didn't believe me"

BERNARD CRIBBINS, *RT DECEMBER 2008*

IN THEIR OWN WORDS

"If you've emotional stuff to do, you put a hell of a lot into it. If it sticks in people's minds then that's lovely. Especially kids. They call out to me on the street, 'Hello, Grandad!' It's been a smashing time."
RT, December 2009

Russell T Davies: "He's not just there for the comedy. Bernard can break your heart with a look, a gesture, a smile. That's why he's the perfect companion for the tenth Doctor's final tale – two wise old men fighting the good fight."
RT, December 2009

THE MOTT
Above: in *Voyage of the Damned* (2007), Wilf told Astrid (Kylie Minogue) and the Doctor (David Tennant) that London was deserted after a series of yuletide disasters

Right: in *Turn Left* (2008) Wilf was horrified by spiralling events and, as their friends were carted away, the war veteran told Donna (Catherine Tate), "Labour camps. That's what they called them last time... It's happening again."

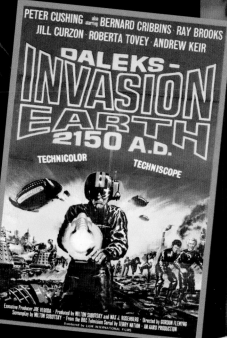

MOVIE MAGIC
Bernard Cribbins (second right) co-starred with Roberta Tovey, Jill Curzon and Peter Cushing in the 1966 Dalek feature film

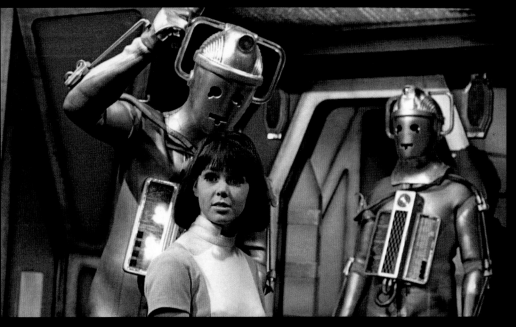

ZOE HERIOT
Wendy Padbury

Dates: 1968–69, 1983
Doctor: Patrick Troughton

This brilliant and ultra-sensible 21st-century astrophysicist stowed away aboard the Tardis to broaden her intellectual and emotional horizons. Her actions were often governed by logic and she once boasted, while referring to the Doctor, "He's almost as clever as I am." Together with Jamie, Zoe was returned by the Time Lords to her own time and place, her mind wiped of all memory of her Tardis travels. She returned briefly as a phantom in *The Five Doctors* (1983).

IN THEIR OWN WORDS

"It's very scary and exciting, but I'm loving it."
RT, August 1968

"She was originally intended to be a computerised type of lady without many human emotions. But it didn't take long for her to become a gibbering wreck, screaming in the corner like everybody else. It was super to work with Pat Troughton and Frazer Hines. Patrick had been my favourite actor since a child. My mother and I were potty about him. He's got such a fantastic face. Once, at rehearsals, Frazer and I debagged Patrick in the Tardis and sent him out trouserless! The three of us all left together. What a sad day!"
RT, 10th Anniversary Special, 1973

"I was Zoe, an astrophysicist found on a wheel in space. I was supposed to be brainier, but after three episodes I was screaming as hard as the rest. I was meant to be fairly trendy, but had no sex appeal at all in the series. I was just a young, terrified girl, the last of the naive ones. They're much better now."
RT, September 1978

"It was the happiest job I've ever had. Doing *The Five Doctors* and meeting up with Patrick and Frazer again was marvellous. We were as silly as ever."
RT, 20th Anniversary Special, 1983

"Zoe, unlike a lot of my predecessors on the series, was very intelligent and capable of pointing things out to the Doctor. This made Jamie look very thick as Zoe and the Doctor compared notes and he would just go, 'Oh, och aye' now and again."
RT, May 1996

21st-CENTURY GIRL
RT visited the Tardis set and caught Wendy Padbury in her sparkly, catsuited glory as Zoe (*The Mind Robber*, 1968)

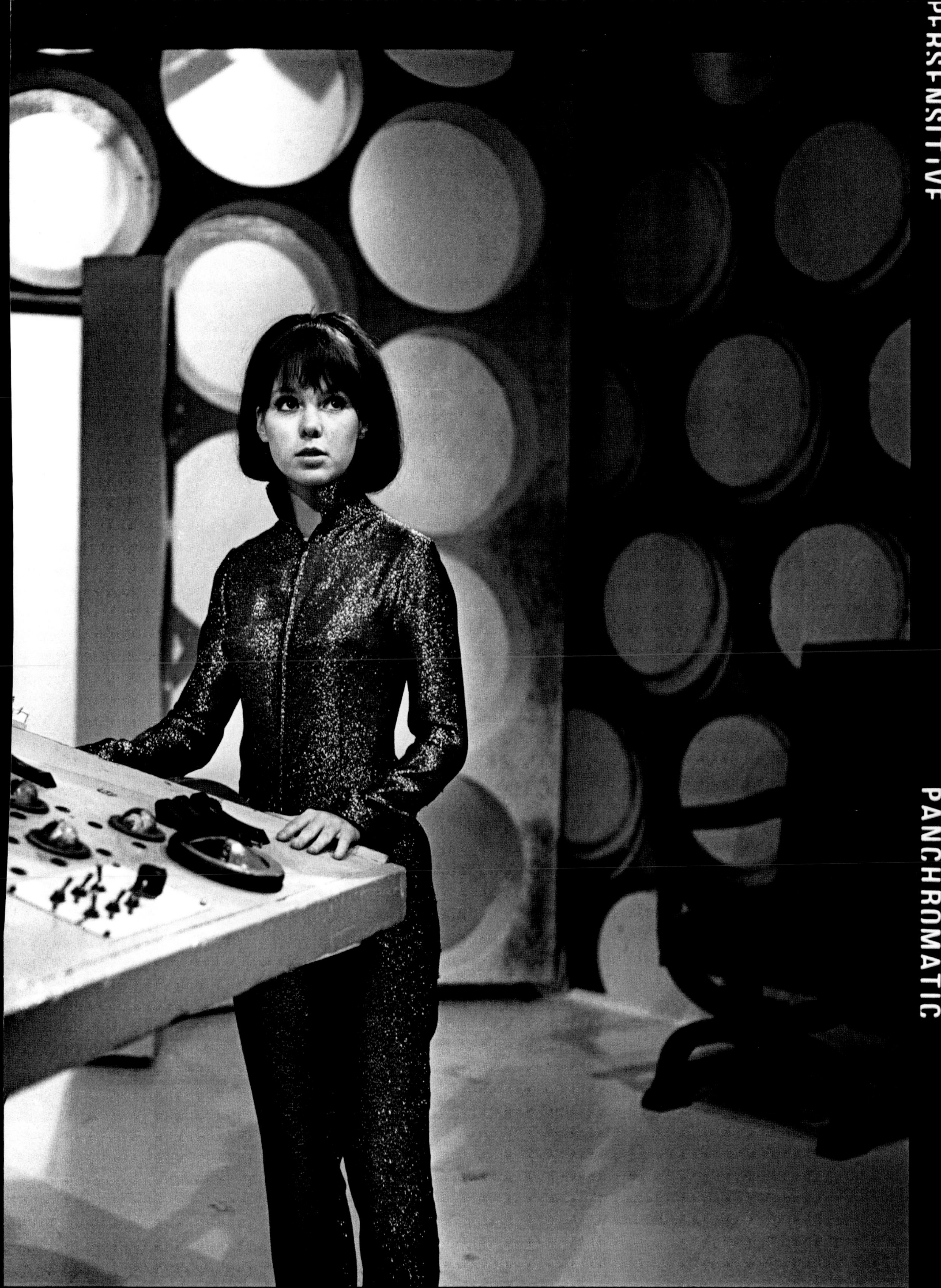
PANCHROMATIC

SELECTED FEMALE, ZO-GOND
In the Gonds' Learning Hall, Zoe surpassed the scores of all former students, to which the Doctor responded, "Zoe is something of a genius. Of course it can be very irritating at times!"
(*The Krotons*, 1969)

MELTDOWN
"Print out Y to the minus X variable one... Now, continue, print out continuous integration."
For *RT's 10th Anniversary Special*, Wendy Padbury re-created a scene from *The Invasion* five years earlier when Zoe blew up a computer with an insoluble equation

MEMORABLE MOMENT
The cerebral scientist goes all kick-ass (literally) when she grapples the Karkus, a comic-strip character brought to life in the Land of Fiction. She boots him up the backside and puts the exhausted superhero in a headlock.
(*The Mind Robber*, 1968)

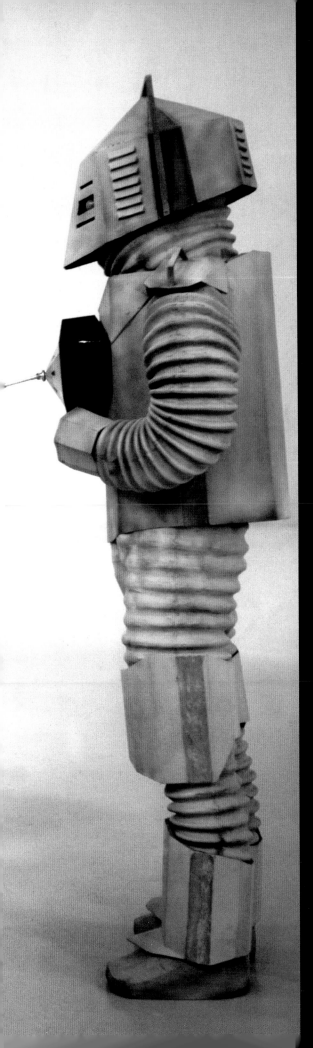

"*The Mind Robber* was my favourite story. It was very different from any other. It was so innovative and I just loved that"

WENDY PADBURY, *RT November 2003*

RadioTimes
THE COMPANIONS

Credits

Design and art direction Paul Smith
Researched and written by
Patrick Mulkern and Mark Braxton
Design Stuart Manning

Editor Ben Preston
Commissioning editor Anne Jowett
Picture editor Roger Dixon
Head of heritage Ralph Montagu
Repro technicians Martin McCormack, Ian Crabb
Production controller Steve Calver
Publishing director Kathy Day
Publisher Zoë Helme
Printing Ancient House Printing Group, Ipswich

Photographs copyright _RT_ and BBC
_RT_ **staff photographer** Don Smith
Other contributing photographers include:
Sven Arnstein, William Baker, Allan Ballard,
Dan Goldsmith, Mark Harrison, Mike Hogan,
Matt Holyoak, Ian McKinnell, Perou, Chris Ridley,
Adrian Rogers and John Timbers

Additional images
Patrick Mulkern (page 52), Rex Features (page 75),
PA (page 113), Allstar (page 155)

_RT_ **interviews by**
Anwer Bati, Johnny Black, Mark Braxton,
Benjamin Cook, E Jane Dickson, Andrew Duncan,
Geoff Ellis, David Gillard, Alison Graham, Katy Griffiths,
Nick Griffiths, Liz Hodgkinson, Deirdre Macdonald,
Christopher Middleton, Steve Morrissey,
Patrick Mulkern, Vicky Payne, Gary Russell,
Gay Search and Michael Wynn Jones

With thanks to
The cast and crew of _Doctor Who_ past and present.
Waris Hussein and Derek Handley

Published by BBC Worldwide Ltd, Media Centre,
201 Wood Lane, London W12 7TQ
© BBC Worldwide Ltd 2010

So who is your favourite companion?

When we heard Jo Grant was dropping in on _The Sarah Jane Adventures_ in October 2010, it seemed the perfect time to ask _RT_ readers to name their all-time favourite companion – and you responded in your thousands. Back in 2003, Sarah Jane Smith came top, with K•9 hot on her heels, but that was before the new _Who_ crew had hit our screens...

01 **Rose Tyler**
02 **Sarah Jane Smith**
03 **Donna Noble**
04 **K•9**
05 **Amy Pond**
06 **Captain Jack Harkness**
07 **Ace**
08 **Leela**
09 **Jo Grant**
10 **Brigadier Lethbridge Stewart**
11 **Martha Jones**
12 **Jamie McCrimmon**
13 **Romana II**
   Tegan Jovanka
   Wilfred Mott
14 **Peri Brown**
15 **River Song**
16 **Harry Sullivan**
   Polly
17 **Turlough**
18 **Nyssa**
19 **Zoe Heriot**
20 **Romana I**
   Rory Williams
21 **Ian Chesterton**
22 **Barbara Wright**
23 **Liz Shaw**
24 **Vicki**
25 **Lady Christina De Souza**
26 **Victoria Waterfield**
27 **Katarina**
28 **Adric**
   Mickey Smith
29 **Astrid Peth**
30 **Captain Mike Yates**
   Mel
   Susan Foreman
31 **Grace Holloway**
32 **Ben Jackson**
   Dodo Chaplet
   Steven Taylor
33 **Sara Kingdom**
34 **Jackie Tyler**
   Sergeant Benton
35 **Adam Mitchell**
   Captain Adelaide Brooke
   Jackson Lake
36 **Kamelion**